SOUL MISSION

LEADERS USHERING IN THE NEW EARTH

JESSICA VERRILL   LISA ZOE MORGAN

ANDREA GREINER   CORNELIA HELGA SCHULZE

DR. ERICA PEABODY, D.C.   LELIA CEAUSU

DOMINIQUE DIDINAL   DR. RACHEL KAPUSTKA, D.C.

TINA D'AMORE   AMANADA SULLIVAN

BRITTANY YOUNG   KELLY KINGSLAND

SANDRA JOY LARATONDA   EVA GOULETTE

KATHERINE M. DEAN   SHANNON A. FISHER

TIFFANY MCCOY   ELISSA NAUMAN

KALAIN HILDERBRAND   DESIREE BARTON

HANNAH WATSON   ADAM MENDOZA

HOUSE OF INDIGO

DISCLAIMER

The publisher and the author are providing this book and its contents on an "as is" basis and make no representations or warranties of any kind with respect to this book or its contents. The publisher and the author disclaim all such representations and warranties, including but not limited to warranties of healthcare for a particular purpose. In addition, the publisher and the author assume no responsibility for errors, inaccuracies, omissions, or any other inconsistencies herein.

The content of this book is for informational purposes only and is not intended to diagnose, treat, cure, or prevent any condition or disease. You understand that this book is not intended as a substitute for consultation with a licensed practitioner. Please consult with your own physician or healthcare specialist regarding the suggestions and recommendations made in this book. The use of this book implies your acceptance of this disclaimer.

The publisher and the author make no guarantees concerning the level of success you may experience by following the advice and strategies contained in this book, and you accept the risk that results will differ for each individual. The testimonials and examples provided in this book show exceptional results, which may not apply to the average reader, and are not intended to represent or guarantee that you will achieve the same or similar results.

CONTENTS

FOREWORD

Being on a soul mission may be something we quickly identify with or it could be a new term to us. Simply put, it is the knowing and feeling that we are on this earth, at this time, for a purpose or mission, one of our soul.

Often we feel the pull, we know we are being led to something, that there is something within us that is here to create change, impact or help others. It usually eludes us for some time until we are faced with opportunities to transcend, grow, heal and go inward; either by external or internal circumstances.

A new earth is spoken of in terms of a new consciousness where our collective relating, being and doing are that of a unified sense. Many of our current systems, thinking and experiences that have a hierarchal sense or those impending any freedoms, will shift. Many are or will experience spiritual awakenings for this to be created.

The contributors to this collaboration all know they are here on a soul mission, one ushering in a new earth, and are sharing their stories of the changes they have personal faced in coming to their current perspectives.

This book will serve as a resource for transcending mindset, energetic and relationship beliefs. Simply put, it will shift your approach to business and life. Put into practice the tools, techniques and lessons presented before you. For a deeper dive, all contact information is in each author's biography.

This book was divinely created and guided. Everything from the cover image to the theme and amount of contributors was a co-creation between the publisher and her spiritual guides. You are exactly where you are supposed to be.

Thank you in holding this vision of a new earth with us, wherever you are on your journey. We honor you, we appreciate you and we send you love.

Jessica Verrill, Founder of House of Indigo

LISA ZOE MORGAN

THE WAY OF THE FEMININE IN BUSINESS

I didn't know what was happening.

One minute I saw myself standing on top of a mountain, on what looked like a cross-section of earth.

There was a gigantic crevasse running up through the middle of it.

The next, I felt the whole planet reverberate through my body.

I realised I was dreaming.

It was one of those dreams I have, where I know I'm dreaming and decide whether I want to wake up or not.

When I'm in this brainwave of sleep, I get really clear answers to any questions I ask.

So, curious as to what the hell just happened, I decided to stay there and ask.

I heard back, "The earth just shifted timelines."

"Why?"

"Because it was about to end."

I slowly opened my eyes, shocked, feeling the magnitude of this answer.

It happened in the lead-up to the elections in the US.

Where the chaos, fear, and uncertainty were palpable in the air.

Whether the earth was on track to end or not doesn't really matter.

It didn't.

What does matter is our new earth.

That it thrives.

And each and every single one of us does our best to create a place that's as harmonious as possible to live on.

For some, that looks like working with climate change.

For me, it looks like working with women to help bring the feminine energy back into the world.

Into their work, their lives, their body.

It was never completely lost.

It just got stuffed down with patriarchy.

This chapter is a story of how my own masculine energy took me to a dark place.

It's a story of my first wake-up call.

A call I couldn't ignore.

That had me return back to who I was at my core.

The person I'd ignored.

My feminine.

This led me to my soul's true path and purpose.

A whole new way of doing life (and business).

It was a long, arduous journey to get here.

One that doesn't have to be this way.

I'm extremely grateful for it, nonetheless.

As I now know, deep within my bones...

Just how important the feminine is.

For me.

For you.

For the world.

I hope you get a sense of this too.

First, a little background.

There's a quiet revolution taking place in the online space.

Female coaches and soulful entrepreneurs are making millions online and impacting millions of lives.

These are my people.

I'm one of them too.

Before this, I was a die-hard scientist working as a Radiographer.

Working in hospitals is a far cry from working online, where we get to do biz our way, on our terms.

Here we get to share our unique gifts on a huge global platform.

Gifts that would have had us previously locked up (or burnt at the stake even) had it been a different era.

They're incredibly potent and important.

Why would anybody have bothered if they weren't?

This sharing of gifts, talking openly about them, and owning them is one part of women reclaiming their feminine again.

The other part is women being more in their feminine energy at work, in a world that's predominantly been masculine-driven.

We've all been conditioned by the patriarchy.

I grew up believing that I had to work hard to succeed, so I did.

The continuous pushing to get work done was me heavily in my masculine energy.

What I didn't know back then was that when a woman combines this masculine energy alongside the feminine, work feels good.

Rather than it feeling like a battle.

Online, this is when business booms!

The whole world benefits too.

Because a new paradigm of working is created. One that embraces both the masculine and the feminine.

It shows other women there's a more aligned way for them.

We can finally relax and breathe.

———

If you're not so well-versed in the energies of the masculine or feminine, here's a little riff.

The feminine energy got stuffed down when women went into the workplace.

They wanted to prove they were smart enough, could do, do, do, (just like men), were strong enough, logical enough, and could find solutions to problems too.

Masculine men thrive in these energies.

Whereas women don't for long periods of time.

Put simply; masculine energy is one of penetration.

Feminine energy is one of receiving.

Expression. Feeling. Being, more than doing. Vulnerability. Intuition. Heart over head. Relationships over competition.

It's a much more playful, soft energy, where the process is enjoyed, not just the outcome.

If you're cringing as a woman reading some of these qualities:

I want to remind you that through the first wave of feminism and women in the workplace, we learned and proved we can do all of these things a man can do.

But just because we can doesn't mean we should.

This was (and is) us valuing the masculine qualities over our feminine ones.

We've been conditioned to believe they're more important.

When we start to tap into and value our own feminine, we see what true equality really is.

Equal and opposite to masculine energy.

Just like the yin and yang symbol.

They work perfectly together.

Neither energy is better, just different.

The suppression of the feminine energy has been going on way before the workplace, though.

Think organised religion and witch trials.

Even before this, in ancient civilisations, such as Atlantis.

We have no proof that Atlantis existed, yet the feminine journey is about learning to trust what she knows without proof.

Whilst evidence is completely valid and necessary, our knowing as a woman is too.

Our world values science, yet science doesn't have all the answers.

When I got sick, I didn't get the answers from science.

So I improvised. I turned elsewhere. I had to let go of everything I thought I knew.

I wouldn't be here today if I needed proof of my recovery.

Because there wasn't much out there.

Experiences like this really strengthen my feminine.

Through my own work, I've found the amount of feminine energy differs from person to person.

One woman can naturally have a lot more feminine energy than another.

Sometimes, a woman will naturally have more masculine energy than feminine or vice-versa.

Whatever energy you naturally run will feel the best for you.

In my business, I work best with roughly 80% feminine energy and 20% masculine.

This chapter you're reading will be just 60% feminine and 40% masculine.

I know there'll be a reason for that, based on the transmission through these pages and who's reading.

The world is always in relationship.

The feminine is a part of that world that hasn't fully been unleashed yet.

This is not about denying your masculine but tapping into something that's been buried under years and years of conditioning.

In a way, we're reclaiming the feminine.

Allowing it to shine through.

It's not about dressing prettier, making your biz prettier, or feeling less guilty about having more rest.

Although that can be a small part of it.

It runs way deeper.

In just your business, it can become the difference between night and day when you start tapping into this source.

Just talking about it here is masculine.

You have to truly FEEL it.

Embodying it is feminine.

Business will suddenly become way more fun.

You might have had this happen in your biz before, where you attracted a client, and it felt so easy.

Then maybe something kicked in, and you were afraid if you didn't do, do, do again, your business wouldn't grow?

I was talking to my client recently, and she was telling me how clients are just finding her without doing much.

People are talking about and sharing her work.

To see the ease in her face and body as she told me this is what it's about. Enjoying being in this space.

Things do move here, but it's not about exertion.

A few weeks earlier, she was pushing for clients.

And yes, the push can be the masculine fire to get things moving, but doing this continuously was not sustainable for her.

We did the inner work to get her to a place where she could trust there could be an easier way.

In this place, intuitive strategies can drop in without too much thinking.

My client began to send videos out to her potential clients rather than jumping on calls with them.

She had her highest ever month working this way, then broke through to a 5 figure month.

Before we started working together, she didn't even know she was in the wrong niche.

We cleared fears and connected her back to her body and the knowing of what she was here to do.

Then everything clicked into place.

She stepped into a bigger playing field.

Ideas came, inspiration, next steps became obvious.

Clients came.

This is the magic of the feminine.

We make things so hard.

Conditioning telling us to put in the effort in case business stops.

What if it could be different?

I had another client landing an inbox of potential clients from a post she felt compelled to write.

She'd been overthinking posts before and trying too hard.

It gets to be easier, if we just let it.

Fears are naturally going to come up.

Our feminine requires trust and surrender.

The work that gets you here is inner work, not hard physical work.

The mindset shifts, finding and clearing beliefs, fears, blocks, the energy work.

Receiving states.

Slowing down enough to hear the intuitive whispers (that might land you your next client.)

The feminine knows.

Once the armour drops, we access that soft core.

Our gifts. Our intuition. Our magic.

You also connect to the universe on speed dial.

What more could you desire?

Enjoy the process.

As we move forward into the new earth, you're going to see the older masculine ways fall away.

As long as you don't keep feeding them.

It's already happening as we speak.

There's cracks in the structures and systems.

Remember the dream I spoke about?

As the energy of the earth (and our body) becomes more refined as we evolve, the change will become easier.

You'll simply no longer be able to operate in the old ways as much.

They just won't work as well for you.

Marketing and selling will move from a more fear-based model, to one of trust and co-creation.

You'll be called to find a new way.

The more you connect to yourself, the more you'll know what feels good in your business.

Strategies, services, pricing, decisions will become clearer.

Women will attract their soul groups for collaboration.

You'll start trusting how important the feminine energy is as we move forwards into the new earth.

It's going to be your guide.

Your feminine was never wrong.

It's who you are.

Now it hasn't always been easy for me to connect to my feminine.

Somewhere on the path to adulthood, I decided to reject it.

Then after ignoring the whispers of her wanting me to acknowledge her, she got louder.

Around 2003, my boyfriend and I at the time planned a trip to travel the world for six months.

Our plan was to start in New Zealand (where he was from) via Rarotonga, then on to Australia, and finally India.

By the time we arrived in Rarotonga, I'd been through so much emotionally and physically the previous few months.

I'd been working hard and also had an unexpected termination.

Looking back now, I grieve for that girl I was there, so disconnected from how she felt.

She pushed through it all.

Yet, my body was obviously processing it all when I arrived in Rarotonga. I had a mild chest infection and didn't feel great.

By the time we got to New Zealand and then Australia, I still wasn't one hundred percent.

I was getting tired after long hikes. The kind of tired where I couldn't keep my eyelids open.

I knew something wasn't right, but I thought I'd be ok.

I always was ok. I soldiered on.

India was next on the list. I felt apprehensive, just because it was so different from what I had experienced before.

Spirituality, religion, death, all these things terrified me, and I knew I'd come face to face with them here.

Walking the streets of Varanasi, dead bodies were carried past us, taken to the river Ganges for ceremonial burning.

I was having vivid nightmares.

My nervous system was buzzing.

Then one day, on a train, I had a man throw a snake in my face.

I was terrified.

Like always, I pushed down what I was feeling.

But it was before Varanasi where it happened.

We were in Agra.

As my ex was organising hiring a motorbike from the cafe owner where we'd just had lunch, I went for a walk around town.

I started to feel faint, and my eyes were blurring over.

I went back to the cafe, and they took me onto the roof, where there were cold showers.

As I put my hand in the water, I got pins and needles shoot through my arm. My body went into rigour. My arms straight by my side, shoulders up next to my ears.

They rushed me to what we thought was a hospital on the back of a motorbike.

I thought it was my last night alive.

Somehow it wasn't supposed to end that way.

I had dengue fever, possibly. Malaria. Nobody knew. But I stayed there as they pumped me full of drugs.

The cold water was spitting out from an old-fashioned air conditioning unit in front of me, as I was hallucinating.

The doctor told me to 'pray to God' when all I wanted was some good solid medical advice.

After about a week of me being there, we left.

I wasn't even in a fit state to even carry my rucksack.

So after Varanasi, we cut the trip short.

I felt relieved to get home, but things got much worse.

Now, I could barely speak or move.

The doctor said I had post-viral fatigue, and it might take two months, two years, 20 years to get better or that I may never recover at all.

All the medical tests came back negative, and I ended up mostly bed-bound for years to follow.

I'd trusted the medical field with my life, and it felt as if it had failed me. I went through what I now know as the dark night of the soul.

There was no further way down from here.

So I began the long and arduous journey back.

I'd gone from 90 hour work weeks, partying with friends most weekends to this.

And 'nothing' wrong with me.

I felt alone. Invisible. Like I was slowly dying, and nobody knew why or when this torture would end.

I just wanted my old life back.

Yet that old (masculine version of) me was dying.

Peeling back the layers to my true (more feminine) self.

Just like what's happening to the earth right now.

I had nowhere to run to as this happened.

No parties to go to, no alcohol to drink, drugs to consume, work to do, or people to meet.

Just me, in bed, 24/7, with my thoughts and feelings.

I was faced with myself for the first time in my life.

My body wouldn't move, yet the days where my head was clear left me with the painful reality of my situation.

Over time, I had to learn radical surrender. Accepting myself and my life at this moment, then the next.

I had to let go of all my future plans, not knowing if I'd ever leave my room.

Meanwhile, within me, there was a tiny flame still flickering.

It never quite went out.

I trusted that somehow, despite the odds, I'd get better.

I was drawn to spiritual and personal development books. If the medical profession couldn't help, I needed an alternative.

Most days, I could just read a line or two before I got exhausted.

I started talking to angels and spirit guides to ask for help.

I had nothing to lose anymore.

As I lay in bed, I'd imagine myself running through fields, just to feel less trapped in this body.

All of this started opening up another world.

One I wasn't familiar with but felt more so when I got into it.

A world of subtle energy.

I became highly attuned to what gave me energy or took it away.

Which thoughts and feelings even.

And as time went by, I started to put my newfound practices to use so I could leave the house.

I learnt how to maintain a calm energy state whilst focussing only on positive thoughts and listening to my body.

I felt my body pulling me in certain directions, one day to a shop where a woman gave me a Reiki healing session.

After these sessions, I was able to talk a bit more.

This woman later trained me in Reiki so I could use Reiki to heal myself.

Her words ring through my ears right now because she told me I would be writing books in those sessions.

This gave me that glimmer of hope I needed. Imagining one day, I'd be sitting here, writing.

It was a time of great reflection.

My life had been so out of balance.

The working, the pushing.

Ignoring my feelings and body.

Finding it difficult to receive help or support.

I brushed issues under the carpet instead of dealing with them.

But over the years, I made progress.

I trained in energy and psychology-based therapies such as NLP, Coaching, Hypnosis, EFT, SRT, Theta Healing, and Kinesiology to help me get better.

I never returned to the person I was before I got sick. Instead, I feel like I'm kind of a 2.0 version now.

I learnt how to shift beliefs, clear fears, emotions in seconds because I had a lot of work to do.

I learnt the shortcuts but found solace in the journey too.

I was open. I received new tools and techniques from spirit.

I connected back to me.

To my feminine.

I found I was actually a good person.

I saw how I'd bulldozed her by not listening to her or caring for her the way she wanted.

I saw how being distracted from who I was sent me further away from my purpose.

You become numb. To yourself and life.

I didn't realise that this connection is what brings true happiness.

It's the best relationship you can have.

As difficult as it was to get here, I don't regret any of it.

Because I get to live this life today with all the lessons.

I get to grow my business, be in my feminine, and play here.

I found my purpose.

Now I get to help other women experience growing their business without the hustle too.

I see them expand into the woman they're here to be.

Beneath the layers.

Really enjoying this feeling and the results it brings.

Not only in business, but in life.

That feminine energy oozes out.

This woman changes lives through her **BEING** more of herself.

Armour removed. Sword dropped.

There's no battle anymore.

Your job is simply to be yourself.

Being, more than doing.

This is what actually changes the world.

ABOUT THE AUTHOR

LISA ZOE MORGAN

Lisa Zoe Morgan is a Biz Coach, Visionary + Healer that LOVES to play in the subconscious realm.

Teaching ambitious female coaches how to create wildly successful businesses without trying.

She channels the Goddesses, Higher Self, Guides and Starbeings.

Has trained in multiple modalities over sixteen years, including muscle-testing, then Kinesiology in 2016.

Which she combines with her own channelled technology, tools and techniques to help you shift old patterns and install new programming in just seconds.

You'll find her walking the banks of the Thames in London. Drinking hot chocolate in cafes. Taking pictures of flowers, singing, and wondering when she can dance again.

Website: www.lisazoemorgan.com
Email: lisa@lisazoemorgan.com
Instagram: www.instagram.com/lisazoemorgan
Facebook: www.facebook.com/groups/thedivinesisterhoodgroup

ANDREA GREINER

THE EMPOWERED FEMININE

I am here to guide you into a deeper connection with your feminine, it will be a journey into your pelvic floor, pelvic bowl, and energy centers. This will be a deep embodiment where you heal the generational, societal, & religious wounds, along with the emotional, physical, and spiritual traumas that we have held in our bodies for centuries. Now is the time to release these traumas and come into your embodied feminine.

As a trained naturopathic doctor, acupuncturist, and feminine embodiment activator, I want to show you what is possible through a glimpse into my soul mission and how it revealed itself to me as a way to provide a deeper healing and activation for you. In 2005, after I graduated from my undergraduate studies, I spent four months in Zambia, Africa. I knew that I needed to go to Africa. It was on this trip that a major puzzle piece dropped into my life and my soul mission. During a part of this trip, a dear friend of mine and I stayed at a women's shelter and school where we were able to connect with the local women and travel to surrounding villages. We learned how to make soy milk from soy beans and taught the surrounding villages and communities how to do this for themselves and the families in the villages. We spoke with hundreds of women and helped them brainstorm how they could generate more money for their families and care for the children in the villages. This trip was an incredible experience. We bonded with women that were living the roughest lives I have ever seen. As with many trips to developing countries, I went with the aim to "help", and what I realized is that this trip and these amazing women were really there helping me. Which felt so backward. I felt like I should have been able to do more, be more, support more, give more. I realized that at 23 years old, there really wasn't anything I knew that these incredible women didn't know. They showed me what it was to be a community of women and support the children and women that had lost family members due to HIV and AIDS. I saw how obsolete their health care was and how there was not adequate midwifery support and skills to support laboring women in the villages, and a small seed was planted. I wanted to learn how to deliver babies and come back to these villages and provide a true support of simple tools to help more babies live through childbirth in a place where a simple, clean pair of scissors often weren't available to cut an umbilical cord.

When I returned to the US after a total of five months abroad, I knew that I would find some way to support women. I wasn't sure what it looked like, but my entire life path had changed. This searching led me to become certified as a doula, taking a spiritual doula training at Breitenbush Hot Springs. I flew to Tennessee to take a week-long midwifery course with Ina May Gaskin's team of midwives, even though I had never seen a birth yet. I applied to a highly reputable nurse midwifery program still without seeing a birth, knowing I was competing against nurses that had been in labor and delivery for 30 years. I just kept taking steps in a direction, and then I would be guided to the next step that felt good and aligned at that moment. Needless to say, I did not get into the nurse midwifery program. I was guided to apply to naturopathic school to become a naturopathic doctor and midwife. I can remember the feeling I had when I stepped onto the campus of the Naturopathic School. At that time, it was the National College of Natural Medicine (now it is the National University of Natural Medicine).

The feeling was of being home. The sensation was a tug on my soul saying. "This is it. This is your next step... JUMP" I was not prepared to go to school for over six years to become a doctor and an acupuncturist, however EVERY time I get the sense of home, I would listen, and I always would JUMP.

As I applied and got accepted into the Naturopathic College of Natural Medicine, my journey continued. I trained and studied for six years to become a naturopathic doctor, acupuncturist, and certified in midwifery. While I was in school, I was able to contribute as a student to over 60 home births. My belief in the female body and all the power we have was strengthened and empowered. I learned massive amounts of information on how to naturally support the body's innate ability to heal, and I loved all of it. Those six years were some of my most unhealthy years physically and emotionally. They were also incredibly empowering as I regained what I always knew to be true: WE ARE POWERFUL BEINGS. We know how to heal. We are meant to heal. And that I am here to empower as many people as possible in their healing abilities.

It was in my last year of being in naturopathic school that I learned about Holistic Pelvic Floor Therapy™, created by Tami Kent. I searched out this class because I loved empowering women and their healing journeys. This course taught me the internal landscape of our inner pelvic bowl, our vaginal floor, and all the mysteries and wonders that lay in this area, calling us to be healed. I can remember when Tami came and gave me a session within my own internal vaginal floor, and she could tune in to what was calling to be healed. She talked of spirituality, generational healing, and things that I never thought I would begin to understand and unravel for myself, let alone other people! (Now I am doing this as a distance healing and its effects are incredibly profound!)

I was able to integrate the Holistic Pelvic Floor Therapy™ I learned that weekend while I finished out my doctorate program, in my residency, and my own clinic and the results were incredible. Women were able to heal physically after childbirth from symptoms like no longer peeing when they coughed, sneezed or laughed, pain with intercourse, tightness, low libido, irregular periods, heaviness, and much more! Many women were menopausal and were able to connect back to their bodies in ways they never expected. They were able to orgasm and heal from traumas. Many women were able to feel a deep sense of embodiment and love for themselves. Little did I know where this would take me in 2021; more on that soon!

After graduating from naturopathic school in 2014, I was accepted into my top residency choice. While working for a very busy clinic, I learned a lot about the natural approach to repairing our bodies because this clinic still greatly valued the true naturopathic remedies and medicine we learned at NUNM. I wanted to focus on amplifying my knowledge of our body and how we heal with nature, herbs, and the power of our innate healing abilities that was a key focus in naturopathic medical school. I wanted to focus on true healing with nature, herbs, and the power of what we learned in school. Shortly after residency, I got this highly sought-after job, which paid six-figures, and I did this when I was six months pregnant! I knew that working for an urgent care company would solidify my doctoring skills, and honestly, a part of me needed to prove to others that I was a really good "doctor". As we look back at our lives, we can see areas that we did for others and that we truly did for ourselves. Don't get me wrong, having this six-figure job greatly helped our family, and it was awesome for a period of time. This job helped me really see into the allopathic medical field. I knew what it was like to have fifteen-minute visits. I knew what I was missing by not getting to connect with my patients as deeply as I was trained. I also became really good at identifying true emergency cases and was very solid in delivering incredible naturopathic treatments for viral infections. When this company decided to cut all naturopathic doctors' wages by 30K and gave us 30 days notice, my husband and I decided that it was time to move on and start my own practice.

This is where things continued to get bigger, and my soul path was revealed even more. When I decided to leave this company, I still had an almost 94K position, which for most naturopathic docs, is a great wage. I didn't want a great wage, and I was ready to make a difference in a different way. And I wasn't using my acupuncture degree yet. So, I gave four months notice, which at that time, I had also just found out I was pregnant with my second. While I was still working, pregnant, and with a one year old, I studied for my acupuncture boards. I also started my practice at the same time. This was a major LEAP for me. I didn't know how to run a business… I didn't know how I was going to replace that income. What I did know was that this leap was essential in my growth. This was in 2018. My clinic picked up quickly once I was fully in it, and I was booked out several weeks by the time I had my son in August 2018.

Once I was in my own clinic, I could feel an even bigger pull. I could sense that just being in a clinic was not where I was meant to be. I had an inner tug that was saying, "move online." But I didn't see other ND's do this, so I wasn't sure what it meant. I did see one ND, DC, that was making more of an impact online, so I enrolled in her mastermind. Something that I had never done before. I also invested in a psychic business coach, and during 2019, I dove into my purpose. I dove into my spirituality in a different way, and this paved the way for what was going to come for 2020 and 2021. Through this work in 2019, I realized that something I had felt for a long time was true. I was told by my psychic business coach that I was here to change the health care system. At that time, I didn't know what that meant. I didn't have the perspective I do now, which made it difficult to actualize and trust that where I was and what I was doing was exactly where I needed to be. I also didn't have the physical support I had wished I had from my family or my husband because none of them had had their own business before. My support network felt quite small, which fed into my abandonment story for quite awhile until 2020, when our world as we know it changed. It was like my whole life was waiting for March of 2020.

As we are guided in our soul mission, when we can be truly open to it, it will show us the wild, the amazing, and the infinite possibilities available to us. March 2020… We all know what happened. At this time in my clinic, I had left insurance companies and was a sole cash practice. I had moved two clinics in 2019, and my clinic had slowed down with leaving insurance companies and focusing on cash packages. I was focusing just on Pelvic Floor Packages, which included Holistic Pelvic Floor Therapy™, acupuncture, and use of BEMER during these sessions. I closed my clinic the first week of March and never opened it up again. That whisper of moving online had come to its full fruition. I received a free reading from a mentor that first week of March, and her guidance was to create a form of energy healing incorporating energy acupuncture and that I would create an energy school. Well… Holy smokes. That was not what I was expecting. However, I had been practicing distant energy acupuncture. I just hadn't told a soul. So, when she told me this (by accessing my Akashic Records), it all made sense. I dove in. I created the energy form that next week as I was also a part of a meditation group that I joined in January of 2020 that really allowed a lot of this to drop into my soul and my mission as well. I created Ray of Light Meridian Therapy™, and in 2020 I certified 10+ healers in this energy healing form. I trained in the Akashic Records, and my life expanded in ways I had never expected. My business was 100% online.

The year 2020 will be monumental for all of us in a variety of ways. For me, it was a massive accelerator into ME. Into who I was and am meant to be on the planet. I lost family members, I lost animals, I became pregnant (a complete surprise) in August, and I evacuated our house in September due to massive fires. It was one of the hardest years of my life, and yet, it was so expansive. My soul family arrived, friends came from all over the world, my network grew massively. I was on over ten podcasts and several summits. My message that you are an infinite being and can heal anything and standing in my power that energy healing IS the medicine we are missing was huge. Moving into the energy world with my full embodiment was big because I knew it was what was needed, and I couldn't look back. I couldn't stall and worry what others would think. It was my time to LEAP (again!).

By the beginning of 2021, almost a year after leaving my clinic behind, I started having people ask me if I could do the pelvic floor healing from a distance and if I could do group healing sessions. And the answer is a resounding YES! This is where I came full circle and stepped into Feminine Embodiment and Pelvic Floor Activation sessions, contributing to the healing of high six-figure entrepreneurs and female mastermind groups and accelerating their healing and embodiment. The results are even deeper and more phenomenal than when I was in the clinic. The journey into this was so divinely timed and played out. Integrating this healing with Akashic Record activations to amplify all areas of our lives was beyond what I was expecting for 2021 (and we are just a few months in). As many of you know, we are moving into the age of the feminine; our paradigm is shifting. We will see the patriarchy fall as the divine feminine balanced with the divine masculine rise to create the flow, abundance, and healing that is ready to come with this new era.

So, through my life journey I have shared with you, I wish to leave you with the "knowing" of healing into your feminine and your pelvic floor. And the remembrance that ALL of you knows how to heal. You are an infinite being and listen because your soul mission and soul are calling you. Let's journey there now. Find a cozy place you feel safe and comfortable. I like to light a candle and use some essential oils. Rest one hand on your heart and another on your lower abdomen, and take five deep breaths in through your nose and out your mouth. Create a connection into the middle of the earth and one up to source/god/creator. When I do this, I breathe in the crystalline grid from the center of the earth, and I allow that to integrate into my physical body. I also pour in the divine energy from God/Source/Creator and intermix this within my body. Relax your body from the top of your head to your feet. Then bring your attention to your lower abdomen. Imagine a beautiful golden bowl in this area (a sound bowl or Tibetan bowl is perfect). Then imagine you are in the golden bowl and gently sweep anything that is "stuck" there out of your pelvic floor space and into the earth. As if a cord was leaving through your root chakra and into the earth. Be easy here. Take your time with what you feel in this area. When emotions come up, gently allow them to go down into the earth. Then, allow the image of nutrient-dense mineral water flowing and circling around the bowl, bringing your body all the nutrients it needs into your pelvic floor. The water seeps into all your muscles of the pelvic floor and is absorbed into all of your cells. Allow an image of a flower into this bowl and let that flower stay there and the essence flowing into the water and into the muscles. As the flower essence melts into your muscles, certain memories will come up and be released through the cord into the earth. Connect in with this flower through exploring them as essential oils or flower essences—Journal your experiences. As you notice blockages come up, allow them to flow out of the pelvic floor and into the earth. As you do this each day, you will feel more and more embodied as you create space for more of YOU to join you.

This is just the beginning of your pelvic floor and feminine embodiment activation! We can do this as a group through my group membership or as a 1:1 session. We can heal the religious, societal, and generational programming that is holding you back in this space. We can journey into the feminine and masculine imbalances present in this space to allow more FLOW into your life. As we allow the divine feminine the space it's been crying out to us to embody, we allow in our ability to receive, to BE, and to heal in ways that are miraculous and joyous. Are you ready?

ABOUT THE AUTHOR

ANDREA GREINER

Andrea Greiner is the creator of Ray of Light Meridian Therapy™, a form of energy healing that integrates the activation of your meridian systems. This training allows healers and clinicians to create a business where they can contribute to the healing of others while building their business from anywhere. Trained as a naturopathic doctor and acupuncturist, Andrea, has now moved all of her business online and integrates her knowledge of healing physical symptoms with an energetic perspective, Akashic Record training and her innate medical intuitive skills gained while she has practiced as a naturopathic doctor and acupuncturist since 2014.

Upon creating a certification program training healers, clinicians and leaders throughout 2020 Andrea also intertwined her profound ability of empowerment and specifically female empowerment and allowed herself to deepen and step into becoming a Feminine Embodiment & Wealth Activator. Now she primarily focuses her energy on bringing together leaders, healers and female entrepreneurs into her Ray of Light Group Healing Membership Program and as a high level coach providing Feminine Embodiment & Pelvic Floor Activations for female leaders both in a 1:1 offering and 9 month Embodiment to Wealth and Oneness program. She continues to train and certify healers in the Ray of Light Meridian Therapy™ Program.

Andrea lives in Canby, Oregon with her husband, three bio kids (including a newborn!), two non bio kids, two cats and a dog. She loves being in nature and her garden where she feels most connected to her truest self.

Website: www.drandreagreiner.org
FaceBook: @andreagreiner
Instagram: @drandreagreiner
Clubhouse: @drandreagreiner
*Join Membership:*http://bit.ly/RayofLightMembership

CORNELIA HELGA SCHULZE

HOW TO CRAFT YOUR SOUL MISSION

*P*eople have been in search of their soul mission across the ages.

As a spiritual medium, I find that many people seem to think I know every detail about their past, present, and future. One of the most frequent requests during a reading is "Tell me what my purpose in life is."

It seems many people believe that life is pointless unless you discover the deeper meaning of life. To accomplish this, they say, you have to find your true calling and fulfill your mission. The core message of the mission can be found in many ways, some seek it through the spiritual path. But so often, the mission itself is seen as a severe, mostly selfless, service to save the world. They say it's destiny.

Sometimes we are even told that we "have to find our special gift" to accomplish the soul mission. Which urges me to ask: Does a life mission necessarily require someone to be a spiritual seeker? Is there a general condition that you must have a particular skill, if not a spiritual power?

I cannot say that these ideas aren't true. But as always, it depends on the way you look at it. For me personally, too many of these definitions carry the underlying requirement that you first have to deliver before—perhaps—you might receive something. But what about unconditionality?

Furthermore, there seems to be a common understanding that following the soul's calling is easy if only one knew what exactly the soul mission was.

So it is understandable that many of my clients are deeply worried if they will find and fulfill their purpose. They sometimes silently fear that, if they don't, true joy and abundance will never be provided.

What if they just didn't realize they were already doing all that was necessary, but only they didn't allow themselves to receive joy and abundance? What if their mission wasn't beyond their control but something they'd become familiar with and interact with along the way?

When my clients ask me this particular question on their purpose in life, I pass on the answer that their spiritual guides provide. Very often, my clients aren't entirely happy with the response — not because they learned that there will be a really heavy task to fulfill on one precise day in the future. No. It occurs they're not satisfied when the answer appears to be trivial, or too easy to accomplish. Sometimes they will have already done something like this before. As their mission they secretly expected, accompanied by a little fear, something bigger than life.

Apropos calling. Today I am a spiritual medium with a special calling for contacting souls after death. I'm also an angel medium, a medical intuitive, and a past life expert. As if this wasn't enough, I made my way through many training programs like family constellations, hypnosis, energetic osteopathy and homeopathy, healing techniques, systemic coaching, and more. With most of my clients, I work as a spiritual coach and mentor for those already on their spiritual path.

I learned about my calling even before I had deliberately chosen to go on a quest for it. It was the answer to a question I didn't ask. And in my case, my calling turned out to be a spiritual mission.

The knowledge of that exact spiritual mission came to me even before I consciously knew I had significant spiritual capacities.

But did knowing my calling make it easier for me to pursue it? Looking back, I can see it guided me in how to think and work very differently. It taught me to develop the most holistic way possible to work on myself and guide my clients and students.

But another important insight I got is: there is not just _one_ soul mission. And it's me, myself, who chose the mission in the first place. Not destiny. Definitely not beyond my control.

With so many people asking me to help them find their soul mission, it is interesting to note that my own was forced on me as unsolicited advice.

I happened upon my spiritual calling while on another path—a healing one. Because for decades, all I wanted in life was to be free from pain. Nothing else. Spiritual development was not my intention.

Looking back to my early years, as far as I can remember, I knew that I was different. Only now I understand there were other reasons involved than it looked like in the first place.

As a child, I was introverted, and I loved books more than people. I also was very quiet, but I could still burst out with anger and rage. Other girls my age were pretty and sociable. I wasn't.

The year I turned 16, I had a life-threatening accident at school during the sports lesson. I broke my spine, and my life was never the same again. For some miraculous reason, I didn't end up paraplegic and eventually could move almost naturally again. But still, heavy pain remained. I felt I was different—again. Backpack traveling through Europe, what most of the other teenagers did those days—I simply couldn't. That's only one example.

In the following years, I tried everything that was recommended to heal. Still, my steady companions for the next decade were pain, sleeping problems, and depression. I spent most of the time taking care of my spine—with little success. Eventually, one of my legs became partially paralyzed. With strong willpower and physiotherapy, I was able to avert surgery for almost three years, but sadly I eventually did have to undergo an operation. The pain remained even though I continued to do the "right" things to recover. Then a second operation was necessary.

It seemed quite hopeless until a friend introduced me to Reiki, a spiritual method to transmit healing energy I had never heard of before. The night after my very first treatment, I slept significantly better. It didn't take long to decide to get a Reiki initiation to be able to treat myself. Yet, the outcome was quite uncommon.

A typical part of a Reiki initiation is the cleansing and opening of the particular energetic channels through which the Reiki energy flows. To be honest, it was only six weeks after surgery, and I didn't know much about Reiki. Usually, the opening is all that happens, but for me, more than just the specific Reiki channel unlocked. I realized when I joined a Reiki training group, I was the only student having repeatedly clear visions while giving Reiki to someone else. Again, I felt different, not fitting in. I discovered that even without giving Reiki, I started to hear voices in my head. At night, I now experienced night terrors without remembering what they were about after waking up. This was the beginning of a strange season of new experiences that, at first, I did not understand.

I continued my healing path, but after two years, my spine felt broken as before. I consulted a specialist for a rare physiotherapy treatment. She was recommended to me as simply a physiotherapist, but she turned out to also be a medical intuitive and a medium. Instead of applying the special treatment, she gave me quite a shock when she declared: "You are surrounded by the souls of dead people." That was unexpected—and frightening. At that point, due to Reiki, I'd been a bit into energetic work, but not too deep. What was I supposed to do with that kind of information? I went to see her again. "Why do those souls keep surrounding me?" was the one question I had. That's not normal. What do they want from me?

I was told: "You have the mission to guide souls into the light." As perplexed as I was, my answer wasn't "Come on, you've got to be kidding me?!" and I didn't say, "No, I don't want a mission, especially not with dead people!" My spontaneous response was: "How do you do that?"

At this point, I didn't consider myself being on a spiritual path because my intent was to achieve painlessness - nothing more.

In the meantime, my Reiki friend had experienced more spiritual disciplines, and after hearing my story, she recommended seeing a medium to know more about that "mission." The medium stated that this is a calling not every medium has, and told me to get a special training to become a medium that can contact the hereafter, to be able to fulfill the calling.

This is how I found myself on a serious spiritual mission without having even set the intention, nor having considered myself as overly "spiritual."

As I hadn't asked for a mission in the first place, I wasn't profoundly committed either becoming a medium or to contacting the hereafter. I was somewhat scared. Nevertheless, I decided to learn the technique. But to be honest, I hoped that this would be enough so that dead people would stop gathering around me.

Soon, I was taught how to do "it." During my final exam of mediumship, I experienced something I wasn't prepared for. My teacher wanted the deceased soul I had contacted to share the information on how he died. This resulted in him making me feel his heart attack—physically. I could feel in my chest how his heart exploded as he died. I was genuinely shocked.

After the exam, traumatized, I put that particular skill aside. It was like having a driver's license and not driving a car. Instead, I continued on my healing path which now officially had developed to be a spiritual path.

All the teachers and coaches I had, spiritual or not, I consider as my spiritual guidance. It was quite astounding that so many knew about mediumship, or even practiced it themselves, but couldn't explain some of the basics. To be able to "read" the aura, chakras, hearing messages from souls after death—having visions, being an empath—how does it work? If you had a particular skill, but it wasn't working properly—where to start in order to fix it? Nobody could explain the secret behind spiritual powers precisely. In the end, the lack of answers made me seek them on my own.

Spiritual "powers"—some people would give their lives to have some and master them. Others assume that these are just imagination or magic tricks, if not delusions.

The mysterious nature of spiritual powers has always been a curiosity. Today, however, spiritual powers can be explained by quantum physics, which claims that everything consists of energy and information. The phenomenon's core is called the law of vibration. At the center of everything, atoms are emitting vibrational frequencies that are constantly in motion. This applies to matter as well as to our personal frequencies. For example, it applies to water, as well as to our emotions and thoughts. Everything and everyone can send energetic frequencies out and receive some.

To receive and give intelligible information, you just have to be on the same wavelength. For instance, it is the same with radio frequencies. You can tune into a station for music, a broadcast, or just find static.

This is the secret behind it: Mediums can align their vibrations to others, thus exchanging information, connecting, and communicating. Each medium works with the part of her/his/its energy field that receives the clearest message. This could be their physical body (being an empath), the mental area of their energy field (telepathy), the extrasensory area (being an intuitive), cognitive and extrasensory area combined (being a psychic—able to read minds), and so on. That's how it's possible to communicate with souls, angels, trees, organs, karma: Being on the same wavelength and knowing about it.

The moment a person is aware of having these capacities and knows how to dial in and dial out, it's a free choice for them to connect or disconnect. Shutting all channels down willingly is something not everyone is able to: First, you need to be aware of this phenomenon, and, even if you are, it still can be difficult. Otherwise, there would be way fewer patients in the world diagnosed with schizophrenia.

Some of the many energetic healing methods I tried helped me to understand that the origin of my pain lay on various other than the physical level. Some methods gradually reduced the pain. I could, therefore, personally evaluate some techniques as effective and decided to learn them myself, including other pieces of energy work.

While studying them, I soon came to the conclusion that most of these, in general, effective techniques had significant limitations, or even gaps. None of them could truly provide a bigger picture of a problem. At first, this awareness felt a bit frustrating, if not uneasy, and then I decided to solve these problems on my own. Therefore, I enhanced and combined methods to fill the gaps concerning, for example, spiritual security, to maximize the outcome and make it more holistic, thus more valuable and efficient.

It goes without saying that my spiritual powers grew with the number of energetic methods I learned.

In the meantime, I had started a small spiritual business. However, I actually worked more as a spiritual coach than as a medium for the hereafter, helping my clients pursue goals that weren't necessarily spiritual. For example, I worked with them to help with finding a new or a better partner or a better job. After releasing what kept them being stuck, they achieved the possibility to experience themselves and their well-known qualities detached from their conditioning from previous experiences, even from childhood.

Even though I helped many people to live a better life, I felt a little guilty not to have my explicitly named mission, to guide souls into the light, at the center of my attention, not working exclusively as a medium for the souls in the hereafter.

Sure, I was a certified medium for contacting the hereafter at this point, but I didn't feel as comfortable with that skill as I thought I should. It was only later, after taking time to learn more, that I realized that this intense, unexpected physical sensation during the exam had kept me from opening up with a hundred percent confidence to the spirits after death for a long time.

Nevertheless, my gut feeling, being reluctant to strictly follow that one official mission but more shifting to spiritual coaching, turned out to be right. It only took me a little longer to realize this.

Concerning my personal issues, I captured some milestones, but some big questions of apparently non-spiritual nature remained unresolved. One of them was: Why couldn't I sleep well at night, feeling extremely exhausted after waking up?

Looking back, my journey to resolve this basic problem helped me to better understand my personal life calling. Moreover, it helped me to get another point of view on soul missions in general. Furthermore, it's an excellent example of how many layers a "simple" problem can have. In conclusion, when not being entirely happy with the outcome of a solution, even if you made some progress, it's always recommended to keep digging deeper until everything feels right.

I took an astonishing path to resolve my sleeping issue. One of the many methods I have learned is past life regression. However, thanks to the knowledge I gained through the past life regression training and my further exploration of this topic, I eventually became an expert on past lives.

At the very beginning, when I was exploring my own past existences, I came across a non-terrestrial existence. I immediately knew that this must have been my very first existence. So, I knew long before it had this beautiful name that I was born a Starseed. Back in these days in Germany, that wasn't common knowledge. Starseeds are souls, born somewhere in the Universe, incarnated on planet Earth, mostly intending to help the planet and its inhabitants to heal.

Knowing about my soul's origin had been essential, even though in the beginning, I didn't know where to place this information. It just was.

Subsequently, I collected more information about the soul itself and incarnations. We often assume that the Universe works like this: Some authority up in the clouds provides tasks to fulfill. As we are used to such descriptions from religions, we are quite used to a likewise inner picture. But I can tell that this isn't correct.

Every soul is on the same hierarchical level as the others, and responsible for its own existence. To incarnate as a human on planet earth is a mission the soul seeks of their own free will. Therefore, a soul crafts its mission on their own. Furthermore, we're not on planet earth to complete an assignment. We don't exist to please the Universe. We literally are the Universe, whether being a Starseed, or a human-born soul, or else.

Amongst other insights, being a Starseed substantially explained my behavior as a child, having problems connecting with—humans. Of course, there was more, as everything always is intertwined.

Obviously, this mission to help the planet was slightly different from the one to guide souls into the light. It seemed to be as though I had two missions.

Diving deeper into the soul's general decisions process itself, I revealed something that brought me closer to solving the sleep problem. I'm also a Helper Soul. A Helper Soul in the sense of someone helping freshly deceased souls scattered in panic all over the planet after their sudden, unexpected death, to find the access to the higher level where healing, as well as the possibility to prepare for the next incarnation, is provided.

It's no surprise this service is done asleep. There were many other aspects from past life existences, causing me trouble with sleeping, in addition to the usual things everybody processes at night. But looking at past lives and the soul's decision-making process made the difference in finding the solution.

Yet, my search for clues to solve a non-spiritual issue had been a turning point concerning my entire life and spiritual path.

To know about being a Helper Soul also provided another answer. The legitimacy of my hesitant attitude towards the statement that I needed to become a medium for contacting the hereafter was now proven. No, I didn't need special training. I already accomplished that mission in my sleep.

Sometimes, a basic problem is only a problem. Sometimes, it can be like a puzzle, consisting of different layers that contain numerous solutions.

Years later, I had another epiphany regarding my mission to guide souls into the light. Given the context of having been surrounded by dead souls when the mission came up, both expert mediums assumed that I needed to become a medium to contact deceased souls.

If we look at the original message "You have the mission to guide souls into the light" from a bigger picture: Why must these souls necessarily be dead?

Therefore, not working exclusively as a medium for the souls in the hereafter but diversifying my work was neither a failure nor avoidance, but a manifestation of my soul's mission.

Finally, it was totally clear now that a soul mission must not automatically consist of one single element. And even if it does, there are different ways of interpretation.

The bigger picture is what is necessary. The soul mission is neither one single nor an unchangeable command. To know it and feel happy with it, we have to know who we are and learn how our personal challenges and solutions are intertwined. Then we need to embrace all facets of ourself. And this process takes as long as it takes.

Everything we do is serving our higher purpose. We serve even if we didn't start any particular path in the first place. We serve even when we're stuck. We serve by just being. And the latter is quite hard to understand!

The bigger picture is my way to work as a mentor. Many of my mentees can work with their powers beautifully, but they don't dare to let their light shine as bright as it's meant to be. An essential part of my mentorship is to let them discover their greatness. While we work to find a solution, I let them choose their own interpretation, lovingly supporting them to open up for more possibilities. They learn to approach their own treasure within. I just have to help pull their greatness out of them, and they're ready to acknowledge themselves as leaders.

I can't tell you how awesome it feels to confirm a student with full honesty that there is no difference between their work quality and my own.

Having or not having spiritual power isn't the problem. It's knowledge. The moment we forget that our soul chose its purpose and mission on its own, we're lost. On our way to spiritual expansion, we just have to look back and become aware that we are the only authority in our life. We are not dependent on a higher power. We craft our mission on our own; that is the very reason why we can change it.

It's not a world of sacrifices anymore. This is the age of completion.
Healers, transformers, spiritual coaches, take off your camouflage. Step into your true significance. Become a light leader. Now.

ABOUT THE AUTHOR

CORNELIA HELGA SCHULZE

Cornelia Helga Schulze is a spiritual medium and coach who is an expert at contacting sources in other dimensions. She has created a highly effective method to examine people's aura, body, soul, and karma, as well as a powerful clearing method. Her skills have earned actors, CEO's and artists as clients.

Born highly intuitive and clairvoyant, Cornelia blocked these abilities as a 6-year-old child. Later in life, she was able to accept these wonderful gifts and share it with others.

Throughout the years, she consequently followed her calling to guide souls into the light. As a spiritual mentor, Cornelia today accompanies intuitive newbies and other gifted women, supporting them to embody their spiritual abilities and gain clarity. With her support they can confidently answer the calling of their soul and create successful spiritual leadership.

Cornelia Helga Schulze

Website: www.corneliahelgaschulze.com
Email: mail@corneliahelgaschulze.com
Facebook: https://www.facebook.com/corneliahelga.schulze/
Instagram: @Corneliahelgaschulze

DR. ERICA PEABODY,
CHIROPRACTOR

DON'T DIE WITH YOUR DAYPACK ON

"*D*on't die with your daypack on."

As I was eating a plate of potatoes, rice and chicken with some sort of red sauce for the fifth night in a row, that phrase caught me wide-eyed and almost choking on the forkful of food I just put in my mouth.

I looked over to my tent-mate with wide eyes. I was curious if she heard what I just heard.

As soon as I finished swallowing that bite of food, I whispered to Kelly *"Is she for real? Does she mean that?"*

We were in the mess tent at Kosovo Basecamp on our way to summit Mt Kilimanjaro. We had been hiking for the past five days and ascended from 4,000 ft to 16,000 ft.

The instructions before our summit hike were to meet in the mess tent for dinner and briefing. We were advised to sleep the best we could until midnight when we began our final ascension.

The word "sleep" was just a general idea of what was supposed to happen, however, sleep had been evading me the entire trip. There is a condition known as "High Altitude Insomnia" and it was the running theme for my entire week. When all was said and done, with a ten-day trip including two full travel days, I slept a total of twenty-four hours.

On summit night, sleep evaded me once again, but I let that be of little concern for what was ahead. This was the day. This was the time. This was the place. Our final summit climb was about to happen.

My clothes and gear were laid out prior to attempting sleep. Donning it all when I woke at midnight was simple. Wake up. Get dressed. Go.

We gathered outside the mess tent and retrieved our water. Each hiking day began with three liters of water in our camelbacks and another liter bottle in our packs. All the little nuances of the trip were interesting including packing the bottle upside down. The sub-freezing temperatures of summit night were bound to ice over the top of the water in the bottle. If the bottle was turned over in the backpack, the ice could still form but turning it upright to remove the cap would be water close to the cap, ice at the bottom.

BRILLIANT!

For the trek up to this point, we had six guides for thirty of us. During summit night, we were paired up so each of us had individual assistance.

My guide was a petite man that spoke very little English. We communicated mostly through hand gestures and single word requests; I quickly gathered that he knew more English by ear than he could speak.

We began our summit trek at midnight, in twenty-degree temperatures, by headlamp. There were thirty women each paired up with a guide, hiking up the mountain about two steps behind the next person. The guides would break into song, in their native tongue Swahili, at any moment and the rest would add to the vocals and clapping.

The singing had become part of our days on the mountain and many of us had learned the lyrics and would sing along. At the end of each hike during the days leading up to summit, the crew would greet us at our next camp in song and dance. The level of pain and discomfort from hiking each day, day after day, was very distracting and the dance party would instantly snap us out of our misery.

I remember back to our first day on the mountain. We were taking a snack and water break and I was standing in a group of eight women chatting about our experiences that day. One woman asked "Hey, how is everyone doing anyway?" In round-robin style everyone answered this question. "This is hard, but I am good." "I feel okay, I am ready to finish the day, but I feel okay." "I feel great."

When it was my turn to answer, my exact words were "I feel awful, I am tired, and everything hurts. I am not even going to pretend any of this is okay" …and then the tears began to stream down my cheeks.

That was only day one.

When we arrived at our tent that evening, I remember thinking if day one was that hard, how will I survive the days ahead?

So back to summit night, this is day five and we are beginning our sixth hike. The day started at Kosovo basecamp, 16,000 ft, and would reach Uhuru Peak summit at 19,341 ft.

We all lined up and our spirits were high. In spite of my lack of sleep (again), I was feeling good and strong. Off we went, "Pole Pole", pronounced "Polay Polay", meaning slow and steady.

The strength I felt beginning this night hike quickly diminished. I could feel my body rapidly declining. To distract me from that feeling, I put on headphones to listen to some of my favorite music. I kept my nose down to focus on the three feet in front of me and continued to put one foot in front of the other.

After thirty minutes, I started to get a heat rush, the hot/cold/sweaty/clammy feeling of my body going into shock. I removed my thick goose down jacket, tied it around my waist and continued.

Another twenty minutes passed, the steady and rapid decline of energy and ability to step forward finally washed over me like a tidal wave. I kept focused and tried to ignore the intensity of the feelings I had in my body. I was doing well until suddenly my knees gave out and I dropped to the rocky ground beside the trail.

My guide stopped with me. We communicated as much as we could, and though I always had the opportunity to give up and turn back, there was a deep desire burning inside of me to get to the summit. After all the work leading up to that point, I was not stopping now.

One thing I should mention is that I have a condition called Patent Foramen Ovale. The hole that is between the top two chambers of the heart that is present and useful in utero, never closed for me. Because of this, some of my venous blood shunts past the lungs. Oxygenation doesn't happen completely therefore I have had chronic low blood oxygen levels, hypoxia, my whole life. Now that we were at such high altitude where oxygen is less available, my body was really struggling.

Through the years, I have never let hypoxia slow me down. Although I struggled during every single day leading up to summit night, I pushed through and had enough strength to make it to this point. The strange feeling of my body collapsing caused me to question if I had pushed the limits too far. I feared I would ultimately get stopped in my tracks this final day. UNACCEPTABLE. I took a moment to gather my energy, got back on my feet and began again.

Initially I felt strong… but I quickly declined. I was communicating this to my guide, and he shared that we will be stopping for a group water/food break in just a few more minutes. Once I knew the break was coming, I was able to wrap my head around continuing to put one foot in front of the other.   I was so relieved when the group leader called for that break.

And then it happened.   I had an emergency approaching in my digestive system and I had the choice of getting a bite of food and a drink of water or going to handle my business off the trail.   Of course, the only answer was to go and handle my business.   I will not share all the details but imagine sitting bare-skinned on a lava rock, in fifteen-degree temperatures with the wind blowing.

This is probably a good time to mention that this also marked the fifth day of my cycle.   Managing a period in the middle of all the nuances of the week was "interesting" to say the least.   When you think of how much we rely on the creature comforts of a warm home, hot showers, access to supplies, change of clothes and rest… yup, it was exactly opposite of that.   Plus, by this point I was so anemic my body's ability to distribute oxygen was additionally compromised.

By the time I gathered myself together, the group had finished the break, geared up and was ready to get moving again.   There was not enough time for me to have any water or food.

We were off.   Since my digestive system was feeling better, I had instant strength and was confident in finishing this trek and making it to the summit.

But once again, I rapidly declined. I pushed myself until I was face down on the rocky trail. This time, I crawled off to the side and let the rest of the group pass me. I was defeated.

I took a breather, a little rest and then my digestive system was on the fritz again. This time I committed to ignore it. I took a few deep breathes and got back in the hiker line. I was relieved to hear another water and food break was just ten minutes away.

I can do this, I told myself. I can do this; I know I can.

By the time the group stopped, I had gathered some supplies and repeated the pattern of our first stop. Once again, I found myself having only enough time to take care of business and returned to the group as they were all geared back up to continue making progress.

"Don't die with your daypack on" ran through my head. One of the things our leader told us during the summit briefing was not to be a hero. If you find yourself in trouble, pass the extra fifteen pounds you are carrying to your assigned guide. In this moment, it felt wise to heed her advise. I knew I was in over my head and needed help. The real possibility of dying with my daypack on prompted me to finally pass it to my assistant.

I was frustrated and failing. This was a real struggle but as soon as I entertained an ounce of defeat inside of my mind, my body would choke up and the tears would start. That was not productive and was not going to work because I needed every last ounce of energy and air I could muster.

I had been there before, in a deep struggle. I had been there before and I knew it wasn't going to be the last time. I had learned that if I chose to settle into the suffering, I was going to stop myself in my tracks and have to turn back. The struggle was evident, but suffering or not suffering was a real choice.

This exact same stop-and-take-care-of-business pattern happened four times and, ultimately, I wasn't able to eat or drink anything for many hours. In spite of the intense struggle, there was always a small well of energy I could somehow tap into and keep pushing.

Around 6AM we were nearing Stella Point, which is at 18,885 ft. As we were making our final approach to this milestone, my body was giving me all the signals that I simply could not go on. My guide clearly saw me struggling. We were so close to the top and it became apparent he was committed to doing everything he could to assist me in my goal.

Suddenly he reached for the trekking pole in my left hand and put it in his left hand. He then grabbed my left arm and assisted in lifting it over his shoulders. We became what resembled a three-legged race configuration. Then it was two steps together and stop, lean over my pole and breathe. Two more steps together and stop, lean over my pole and breathe. This is how I (we) finished the final thirty minutes to reach Stella Point.

I am still so very thankful to that man for helping me reach that spot. Now that my digestive system was completely empty, I was able to sit down on a rock and take an actual break. In that moment, the enormity of what I had accomplished washed over me, I got choked up and the tears started falling. I had to stop myself in the middle of that emotion to be able to catch all the breath I could as I was determined to continue. I finally had a chance to grab a couple bites of food and drink some much-needed water.

Although making it to Stella Point is considered a successful summit (and you get the certificate to commemorate your accomplishment), Uhuru Peak stands at 19,341 ft and was another hour hike beyond Stella Point.

I could not imagine being able to go on…but then my food and water kicked in just as a spark of sunlight began to light up the sprawling vista. It was the most incredible and energizing sunrise I had ever seen, even to this day. It amazed me what a little bit of food, water and sunshine did for my energy levels and I got back up on my feet. With renewed energy, I headed towards the final destination. This time I had fuel inside, and I powerfully trekked the next hour right up to the top.

Because of the sub-zero temperatures, the incredibly thin air and the amount of energy it takes to get to the summit, they do not let us stay there long. Get in line for your picture, hang out for the group photo and then turn around and head back to Kosovo Basecamp.

The initial hour back to Stella Point was a solo hour of introspection. It was at that moment that I became hyperaware of the internal voice and the story I was running in my head. I had trained in a high-altitude gym leading up to this trip. I had built strong muscles and brought my already healthy body up a notch with nutrition, rest and supplementation. I have always had an extraordinarily strong "can do" mindset inside of my life which helped me accomplish my goal that day.

But as I made my way back down to Stella Point, I realized the most important part of the entire trek was knowing and trusting that I could struggle, that struggle is a natural part of being human, but that I do not have to suffer. I also thought about how detrimental it would be if my mindset allowed the suffering to take over my body.

I did not realize that through all the training and all the preparation that I had done, mindset was the most critical.

While I was in college and working towards my bachelor's degree and eventually my Doctor of Chiropractic degree, I was also in the fitness industry. I spent over a decade teaching group fitness classes and found yoga. Over the past fifteen years I have spent countless hours inside of a hot yoga studio. I have a world-renowned teacher who encourages his students to "*do something that makes you nauseous every single day*". He also believes that "*every yoga class should be a 'near death' experience*". He never backs down.

Inside of this style of class, it is practiced over and over again to be inside of moments of struggle. We would hold incredibly challenging postures and transitioning to the next in a room that is humid and over a hundred degrees, packed with people. In those moments, it is rare to find a quiet mind that is peaceful and content. Most are trying to figure a way out, to drop down to a simpler posture. But when you are next to another person that is giving all they have, it is easier to stick with it and settle the mind around just being in it without telling a story. It is quickly evident that the negative internal self-talk and the story wastes a whole lot of energy.

Another one of my brilliant yoga instructors approaches class with the concept that if you need to take a break, do so and then "begin again". And begin again, and again and again if you need to.

During summit night, I used the principles I learned through yoga that I could struggle and not suffer, but if I did find myself in a struggle, I could also take a break and begin again.

As I walked the rim of the volcano back down to Stella Point, this lesson was so profound that I began to think across my entire life of being a Doctor of Chiropractic, a health/life coach, a business owner, a homeowner, and a real estate investor, just how much this lesson applies.

Being in the struggle and choosing to not suffer is a principle I unknowingly had based my life on. The experience of the trek helped me bring that to my consciousness and the practical application still serves me well every day.

When I look back on that adventure, I come up with five distinct rules I unconsciously set up for myself to get to the top. I have been honing these in to create laser point focus on the goals I have set for my life right now and moving forward. I also teach these inside of my clinic as I work with my patients who want to level up their lives and health.

1. **Keep your goal in mind but focus on the next right step.** In the case of summit night, I could only see the next three feet ahead, the only part lit by headlamp. The mindset was vastly different waking up in the darkness of the night and not being able to see the summit even if we tried. When we set goals, oftentimes it can feel like there is such a gap between where we are now and where we want to be. The way to get there is one small step, only what is lit by your proverbial "headlamp", at a time. And if a rest is necessary, take it and begin again.

2. Bat for singles. In the game of baseball, everyone in the stands if hoping their team hits home runs. But what often wins the game are many single base hits strung together. It is not possible to always be hitting home runs in life, but batting consistent singles is how points are put on the scoreboard. This applied to every level of the trek and it is also in a concept of "pole pole" in Swahili…which is how they lead all their groups "slow and steady". They told us leading up to the trip that we will be often hiking at a slower than "normal" pace and it will seem dauntingly and frustratingly slow at times. But slow and steady really does win the race.

3. Celebrate the small wins. At the end of every long day of hiking, we would be greeted at camp with singing and a dance party. The guides would break out in "call and answer" style song. No matter what was happening, how sore or miserable the long hikes had become, it was time to sing and dance and celebrate. They did this intentionally to break up the monotony of the struggle, to shift the energy of suffering back to the focus of the incredible present moment…and incredible it was.

4. Mindset is everything. Negative internal dialogue is a waste of energy. No matter how hard any of it became, the group was moving forward and making progress. Once we got on the mountain the first day, there was not really a way to turn back except in case of emergency. The options were to move forward with an enthusiastic mindset or move forward with resistance, and the latter was a waste of energy. There are things in our lives that we do not want to do. Get it done anyway and drop the negative dialogue about it. When the story stops, the task at hand usually seems simpler and easier and is completed more efficiently.

5. LIVE FULL OUT!!! I was invited on this trip by Kelly, who I initially met because she was one of the patients at my chiropractic office. Somewhere along the way I had tuned my life to seeking out rich and rewarding experiences. If I could safely say "yes" to invitations that were thrown my way, in all areas of life, I would. And I did. Saying "yes" has led me to some incredible experiences, including reaching the "Rooftop of Africa"!!!

The days will pass us all by no matter what. We will come to the end of our life sooner than we imagine. As we can all tell, the energy of our New Earth is shifting in such major ways. While we are here, we may as well step into our greatness. Let's seek out ways to, instead of just GETTING THROUGH OUR DAYS, lets become the people that GIVE TO OUR DAYS!!!

We only get one chance....

ABOUT THE AUTHOR

DR. ERICA PEABODY

Dr. Erica Peabody has a thriving family chiropractic office in the heart of Fenton, Michigan where she has been "Serving the Exceptional Chiropractic Experience" since 2005. She is passionate about sharing health and wellness principles with Fenton and the surrounding communities as well and sharing far and wide though coaching, social media and her blog she has been writing for over a decade. She is an active member in Michigan Association of Chiropractors and the International Chiropractic Pediatric Association.

She has built her dream practice and dream home in Fenton, close to her family, and works hard to squeeze the most juice out of each day. She is an avid yogi, has completed yoga teacher training, has developed a progressive class called "Movement as a Prescription", since she uses yoga inside of her chiropractic practice to help patients heal from many ailments.

When she is not in the practice or at a yoga studio, she can usually be found outside enjoying nature during all four seasons; her favorites are snowboarding in winter and wake surfing in the beautiful Michigan summertime. She is usually reading and writing and on a continual search for the meaning of her life with her Bernedoodle, Louis.

Website: www.cafeoflifefenton.com
We Only Get Once Chance…

Blog: www.fentonchiropractor.org
Facebook: Erica Peabody DC
Instagram: @drericapeabody
Youtube: Dr Erica Peabody, Chiropractor (there is a short vlog documentary of Kilimanjaro)
Email: ericapeabody@gmail.com

LELIA CEAUSU

-ACTIVATING THE VALUE OF BEING-

On a hot August day in humid Amsterdam, I was sitting at my white desk, in a warmed-up living room, staring at my notebook and circling around those written words: "I don't know". With each circle I've made, I was hoping that an answer would be given. As I was sitting alone in that total silence, holding my forehead into my palms, I felt the sweat coming down my spine, burning my skin like a fire.

I had just finished the session with a mentor that I've hired to help me grow my coaching business. After multiple financial investments of almost ten thousands of euros each, in mentorship and coaching courses, putting all my time and energy into my work for the past nine months, I had reached an unbreakable money ceiling and felt stuck. The results I was seeing were almost nonexistent compared to my investments and my impatience started to grow. It had been five months since I had enrolled my last "dream clients" and despite all the smart business strategies and marketing I had in place, according to my Excel spreadsheet, I was almost broke financially and very close to burning out mentally. Things just weren't growing.

I felt that I was playing so small compared to what I knew I could achieve. If my potential was an invisible ball, I'd be sitting somewhere on the sidelines, struggling to find the way to my own centre.

At first, I tried to fix this blockage by waking up an hour earlier but I constantly added more hours to my working days until I reached a point where I was working more than sixty hours a week, which meant I was working more time than back in my corporate days! Skipping the time off on weekends became my new "normal" lifestyle.

Despite all the stress, this was the only success recipe I knew for all my life: if things don't go the way you want, work more, push harder, make sure you don't miss out on things. Everything seemed like a struggle, confirming what I was taught as a child: "Life is hard, don't rush to grow up."

So there I was, trying to grow my business and life was proving to be hard indeed. My magic formula of "do more and you'll succeed" wasn't working for my coaching business. The more I did, the less I saw coming back as a result.

The only result that seemed very predictable if I wasn't stopping this hamster wheels, was to—slowly but surely—burn out.

And I wasn't willing to risk my physical health after spending eight months being sick the previous year, laying in bed and staring at the ceiling most of the time.

So I've hired a mindset and business expert to show me the way out of that stress. I was expecting a breakthrough strategy from her, a quick fix, some changes here and there that would easily multiply my income. At that point, I had changed the process so many times that I wasn't willing to start a new one.

After some strategy and marketing questions about my services and clients, her first advice for me was to step away from my business for a while.

She wasn't worried about my process or what I needed to do more of. She invited me to look at the foundation itself: who was this "business Lelia" I've built, what did I want to create through my work now and what was the energy I was bringing in my own business.

To find the answers that I didn't know, she suggested that I take a break and disconnect completely from any strategy implementation, upcoming launches or projects.

Sitting with my eyes gazed on those words "I don't know", I could feel my chest burning in an inner fire I never allowed myself to express. I didn't know what this fire wanted, what it longed to create. I had been too busy reading emails and working on projects.

I didn't know what my special gifts were, the ones which naturally differentiated me on the business market.
I didn't know where I was going next nor how that next level would even look like.
I didn't know what to do...

The uncertainty that was coming up with this not knowing, was suffocating me.

So I closed my laptop and the notebook with the scary words in it and stepped away from my desk.

I went outside with my husband and sat down on one of the wooden piers, with my feet in the freshwater of the big canal in front of our house.

As I was sitting there and watching the sunset, my mentor's question kept on coming back in my mind:
"Can you BE in this phase- this phase of "I don't know"? Can you learn to BE here?"
"But I don't want to be here", I said while two burning tears came down my face.
In that moment, I heard a voice whispering to me:

"There is value in the being...
Learn how to be. You'll be guided to create a new way, your own
way. Just surrender."

"What's that supposed to mean?" I turned around and realised that
it wasn't my husband speaking to me and no one else was around.
Yet, I was absolutely sure I clearly heard the message.

So I've decided to surrender, to learn how to be and see what kind
of value that would bring. Of course I knew the mindful concept of
"do less, be more", but this time I actually committed to practise it
—every day.

The first step I did was to create space for time off. In that
downtime, my only intention was to find out and reconnect to what
was bringing me excitement. I couldn't remember the last time I felt
pure excitement, the last time I did something just for the fun of it,
without expecting any specific outcome.

I've started to do things that had no value for my busy mind but in
which my soul found joy: playing ping-pong with my husband,
canoeing on the canals around our house, dancing and moving my
body, sleeping until nine o'clock in the morning, reading Rebecca
Campbell's books, writing, or watching cheesy romantic comedies
on TV.

The only connection to my business was reading books in my field
of expertise, my healing work and mindset hygiene I'd do every
single morning.

The second most important commitment I made was to pay
attention and observe my feelings, how I was being throughout the
day, in every activity I had, in every conversation I had, while I was
reading, going for a walk outside, scrolling on my phone or writing.

I used my body's wisdom as my navigation map to discover what
were the activities that had the power to totally reset my mind, to
make me feel enthusiasm and joy. This is how I discovered that
jumping ten minutes on my trampoline, while listening to music,

was the fastest way to shift my energetic state and feel fully recharged.

At the other end of the spectrum, I've also noticed what made my body contract or feel really uncomfortable while resting or doing things that had nothing to do with my work.

There was this nagging voice inside of me (a subtle guilt mixed with judgement) mocking my break moments and running the inventory of all the things I should be doing instead.

I worked on this guilt with Emotional Freedom Techniques* and most of the time I was able to release it from my nervous system. For the remaining parts, I started to keep a journal: **The Value of Being**.

Every night before going to sleep I'd write down the most important things that happened in my breaks, during my sacred time of "do nothing".

---

*Emotional Freedom Techniques (EFT) also known as tapping, is a mind-body technique that has been scientifically proven to effectively resolve a range of issues, including: physical pain release; fears and anxiety about a particular situation; limiting beliefs etc. Instead of using needles (as in acupuncture), the practitioner will use the fingertips to tap on specific pressure points of the body, stimulating the energy system, while verbally or mentally addressing the root causes of distress/ disease.

At the beginning my list had really simple things on it like: being able to release tension from my shoulders, enjoy the beauty of a sunset from our living room, connecting more with my husband during our walks outside, listening to some audio books, feeling recharged after sitting on the beach behind our house.

I've decided that every small thing that brought me some sort of pleasure, joy or relaxation was important enough to be acknowledged and mentioned in my journal, important enough for me to take the time and energy to write it down.

A few days into this process, during one of my relaxation moments, I had a total burst of anger. It was unbearable to stay in that feeling of being stuck and not seeing where this whole thing was going, how this whole "being" state was related to my business growth, making more money, feeling better, serving others.

I clenched my fist and hit the sofa I was sitting on, as if it was the invisible, unbreakable wall that I kept on hitting in my business. In that moment of anger and revolt, a calm voice whispered to me: "Ask and it is given."

It kept repeating its message until I felt called to take my pen and the notebook where the scary words "I don't know" were still circled and started to pour an overwhelming amount of questions on the paper.

I asked all the questions I had about my work, my business, my life mission here, my soul purpose, my divine gifts. And then I waited for the answers.

Silence.
The pen didn't flow, the answers weren't coming.
My mind ridiculed me: "This isn't working."
Yet I was too angry to give up.

I pointed the pen on top of the first question and asked firmly: "Answer me! I ask you here and now to show me the answers. I deserve to know."

And so while I was sitting on that grey sofa that I had been punching a moment before with my jaws clenched from anger, a calm yet ever present part inside of me, stepped ahead and started to move my hand and write the answers. I wrote on and on for ten pages in what became my first ever, written conversation with my soul.

One by one all my questions were answered from a presence within me that I never knew before. This voice had a calm, knowing energy behind and there was a certain depth and wisdom in all those answers that I could have never received from my mind.

At the end of that day, my Value of Being journal had a precious moment to acknowledge: in my break, the anger that was raised inside of me allowed me to tap into the presence of my soul.

The next morning, during my extra hour of sleep, I received the name of a book I was going to channel from the Universe. In the next coming weeks, each time I'd be meditating, listening to a song I loved, jumping on my trampoline, I'd connect to this Divine Source and receive healing methods, meditations, rituals, poems, inspiration. I received constant guidance and soon I started to receive flashes and memories from past lives (being a healer, being a priestess, advocating for people's rights, working with energy, being killed for expressing my truth). Lifetime after lifetime my soul had been crafting my unique set of skills to perfection. That information allowed me to build a deeper connection with my soul, to trust my uniqueness even more and own my power in a way I never did before.

My breaks, my moments of relaxation and pleasure became my divine portal for creativity and inspiration.

In those moments I'd receive full downloads for my business plan, visions of where everything was heading, new perspectives, answers and solutions, directions about who I was meant to serve and how it was all related to my soul's mission here. My imagination became so strong that sometimes a word from a song would speak to me and become one entire page of content promotion.

My list in the Value of Being was growing each day more.

My mind was starting to see, to receive evidence that there was undeniable value in the being. I was starting to learn a new way of being, of creating, of leading my life and business.

My intuition was becoming stronger when my energy was aligned with the frequency of joy, contentment and pleasure. I started to acknowledge how those emotions felt in my body and then I started to declare again and again: "I deserve this. I deserve to live in this state".

And just when I thought that things couldn't get better I went to give and receive a Reiki treatment from one of my friends. I had no particular expectations from that session, just to relax and enjoy it.

As I approached my friend's body with my hands, I felt strong energy being activated in my palms and as I moved my hands above his energetic centers, I started to receive messages from his body about what energy was blocked and where, what needed to be released or changed.

Those messages were very subtle at the beginning: quick flashes of images or words that made no sense, so I chose to ignore them out of fear of *being* weird.

What was I supposed to say: "your chakras are talking to me?".

I pushed the messages away but the energy intensified and my soul spoke to me:

"Tell him the messages. Those messages aren't for you so they don't need to make sense for you. He is the one who needs to know".

So I asked for my friend's permission and started to express the messages out loud.

At the end of that session, I felt so much happiness and contentment for doing this and at the same time, I was shocked by what just happened.

Without me pushing or struggling, it seemed that my divine gifts were emerging and I was starting to awake my own genius power within.

Of course I doubt this! It was all too simple to be true.

I thought it happened just because my friend was highly spiritual so I went home to test this gift also on my husband. In our living room, on our sofa bed, with no special environment, it still worked and I still didn't believe it.

So I decided to face my doubt and chose three strangers, via the internet, to work with them fully guided by my intuition and the Universe.

I did the energy reading of their chakras and all the messages received were accurate. Since I could actually feel their energy I brought into their awareness what was otherwise invisible to them and also what was the actual priority block that needed to be shifted first so that they could move easier in the direction of their aspirations.

Of course I still used the grounded coaching tools and knowledge as before, but I was no longer planning any session ahead. After all, I had the most powerful force guiding me, working through me: the Divine Source. All I had to do was to create the right space for it to come in, to be the right energetic channel so that I could allow it to flow and move through me.

When I stopped obsessing and looking for a solution, my work blockage got solved because I've created space to receive guidance, solutions. Without me intentionally wanting, my work had been taken to a whole new level of expansion and the value I provided was magnified.

The more I stepped into my own power, the more magnetic I became and the easier I could activate the same in all the people that were stepping into my energetic container.

My clients started to experience quantum energetic leaps: standing in their truth, stepping away from toxic relationships that no longer served them, activating their ever fulfilling reserve of energy that magnetized the right community to them, getting the best sleep they've had in years, leading their business with irresistible feminine energy while showing up without apology.

Walking away from my business and surrendering my ways of being and leading it, was one of the hardest things I had to do.

I poured endless amounts of work, energy, money and time to build my business. It wasn't just work, it was my creation, it was part of me.

And the missing piece to my success puzzle, the one I overlooked because—oh well, it was too simple to be valuable—was to invite my own soul to lead my business.

Because spirituality and business seemed two different worlds: one that was meant to exist in the morning time only and the other that was supposed to happen during the rest of the day.

I've completely underestimated the energy of my own being when doing business, because I simply couldn't see how my soul would know the key to making more money. It just didn't make sense to allow something invisible to create something practical.

And yet, my soul set the right foundation for my business and far exceeded my wildest expectations of who I could actually become and the work I was naturally meant to bring into this world. I would have never found these pure golden gifts within me, while I was busy running after the next strategy of growth.

Truth is that we have been so conditioned to do everything for a glimpse of satisfaction and more often than not, we can't even fully enjoy that "successful" moment. Because when it's all a struggle, success just feels like a sacrifice that doesn't pay the equal prize.

If you've seen yourself in my story, if you too were thinking doing more would bring more success, ask yourself to consider this question when you're taking your next sacred break:

"What is the value I've received in exchange, during my break moment?"

Remember to acknowledge every time you feel a state of joy, pleasure or easiness in your sacred moment of break. Write it down.

Create space in your calendar for those breaks of joy. Start to anchor pleasure in your body by consciously choosing an activity or a relaxation moment, just because you know it will feel pleasant and you deserve to feel that joy.

Even if at the beginning it might be subtle, declare every time:

"I deserve to live in this state. I deserve this joy. I deserve this easiness."

If something is blocked in any area of your life, step away from it for a while.

Let it go for a few hours or a few days because when you detach, you open up the sacred portal and you create the space to receive answers. Solutions and ideas you've never thought of before, suddenly start to reveal themselves. They come to you rather than you chasing them.

Besides, when you detach, things no longer seem so serious nor complicated, do they?
Bold ideas no longer seem so out of reach.
The impossible becomes believable.

There is massive value in doing nothing and being more.
It's where your genius power truly awaits for you to awaken it and express it, to allow it to guide you and unlock your true divine potential.

It's in your moments of being when the connection between your body and the pulse of life intensifies: you connect to the space around you, the energy of all that is and suddenly you remember you're not alone, you can receive support and things can actually happen easier.

First of all, BE! And life might surprise you with the rest.

The value is in *being*.

ABOUT THE AUTHOR

LELIA CEAUSU

Lelia Ceausu is an intuitive spiritual leader and certified mindset coach. Through her work she activates the energetic codes of your innate leader so you can rise up and consciously lead from your own unique energetic blueprint.

She is here to activate a quantum leap within you so you can quantum leap your income, shift the energy behind your work and claim -without apology- the space that is truly yours in this world as a sovereign leader.

Trained in NLP, EFT and energy work, she awakens the feminine magnetism within business women so they can stand into their power fully and give voice to their inner fire.

Born in Romania, Lelia currently lives in Amsterdam, NL with her Italian husband.

IG: lelia_c_v
CH: @leliac
FB: https://www.facebook.com/lelia.ceausu.5
Email: coaching@leliaceausu.com
Website: www.leliaceausu.com

DOMINIQUE DIDINAL

THE RADIANCE OF OUR HEART

A week before Christmas in 2012, I found myself staring at the ruinous mass of Angkor Wat in Cambodia. We had gathered on a muddy mound in front of the lake at the temple's entrance to watch the sunrise. Lily pads dotted its surface, a misty haze threaded the air, and the sliver of a crescent moon shimmered in the dawn sky.

Once the sun had risen, I parted ways with my companion and found myself in a secluded part of the temple, undisturbed by any other tourists.

Here in one corner was a taller-than-life Buddha statue. Towering above me, completely unlike other shrines, it exuded an air of rich mystery. All of my senses suddenly felt sharpened, and the lawn outside became a precise grasshopper green.

Unsure of what was about to happen, I found a comfy sitting position on a nearby wall and started to drift in and out of reverie.

My mind wandered to my cousin, Sarah. She was the confident and outgoing sister I had never had, always living life lightly with masses of 'can do' attitude. Three years prior, this healthy 37 year old with three boisterous young sons and a loving partner went to sleep one night and simply never woke up. It was such a sudden blow. Some kind of weakness in the heart—a virus—had been triggered. The kind of virus that ran in the female genetic line but was never mentioned by older generations of women who 'didn't speak of that kind of thing'.

In that suspended state, in the drowsy sunshine, I thought about Sarah. Her death seemed devastatingly senseless. Why had it happened?

Almost simultaneously, as if in response, I received two clear thoughts.

There is a "grand design". The knowing said. We can't question each element because we all have our part to play like the pieces of a jigsaw puzzle. Together, we make a whole, and nothing can be understood separately; it's simply beyond our individual comprehension.

The second image was that of an oyster shell.

Again, a knowing arose. We refine ourselves gradually over lifetimes until the rough scalloped layers of the oyster's lip gives way to the tender, pink shell within and its luminescent pearl is revealed.

When I looked at my watch, I realised two hours had flown past and it was time to meet my companion again.

> *'Who then am I?*
>
> *As a consciousness without origin, not born in*
>
> *time, nor begotten here below. I am that which*
>
> *Was, is and ever shall be, a jewel in the crown of*
>
> *The divine self, a star in the firmament of the*
>
> *Luminous one.'* **Rumi.**

Have you ever done a silent meditation retreat? Do you remember what you looked like at the end? I facilitated them as a meditation teacher in Mexico and people emerged newborn with clear, glowing skin and shining eyes. There was nothing more moving than the final sharing when aspirants allowed themselves to drop the veils of their personality and be witnessed as their raw authentic self, speaking from the heart.

> *'Lovers drink wine all day and night and tear the veils of the mind.*
>
> *When drunk with love's wine, body, heart and soul become one.'* **Rumi**

From the mystics in 13th Century Europe to the Saints of India and the homilies of Western culture —a common thread emerges. It's the wisdom of the heart. We discover that the heart isn't just an organ but our tender emotional self as well as the seat of our soul; it is a divine magnetic portal to a cosmic wisdom greater than us, the unifying field of love. In short, it is our radiance.

Place your hand across the heart right now, close your eyes, and sink into connection with your heart space. Gently repeat the words: I Am. Spend some moments quietly breathing into this deep intimacy with yourself. This is the feeling of 'coming back home'.

I know how easy it is to become disconnected from our heart. It feels like being lost in the wilderness. If that's you, then I want you to know that the truth of your radiance is always there, a softly shining pearl waiting to be uncovered.

The first step is to become aware of our veils.

WITCHES HILL

Not far from where I live now, close to the soft rolling hills and white sandy beaches of North East Scotland, is a hill. It's located in a picturesque little town, the kind you'd visit on holiday for a traditional afternoon tea of scones and clotted cream. The buildings are ancient and beautiful - all large grey stone masonry, with hanging flower baskets and wood beamed pubs.

The hill looks innocent enough but it hides a brutal history. This is Witches Hill.

A little over 300 years ago, women suspected of being witches were pushed into barrels, driven through with spikes and set alight. Then they were pushed (in the flaming barrel) down the hill.

In the dark and suspicious atmosphere of the 17th century, it wasn't just natural healers such as midwives and herbalists that were targeted. The bloody trials were 200 years of fear, torture, and terror that belied a darkly brooding fear of women and 'the feminine' itself as between 3000- 5000 women were forced to stand trial.

Everything that creates the feminine essence—receptivity, intuition, flow of vitality, and sexual energy became despised and mistrusted. The jealousy wound of the sisterhood—women competing against women—had its fans first flamed in those early days of the 17th Century.

Mother-in-laws turned in daughter-in-laws, family members turned against each other, and outspoken women were paraded through the streets in Scold's bridles. There was a clear under-scoring of repressed sexuality. How much easier it was to turn the 'hags' into demons than have the men that accused them confront their own prurient urges.

Is it any wonder that so many women struggle today with owning their voice, allowing themselves to be seen, and feeling safe enough to revel in the vitality of their own sexuality without shame? The past lingers today and those strains of psychopathy, aggression, and dominance have come to define what power is for many of us growing up in a patriarchal society.

Like so many other individuals who suffered at the hands of this 'power over' paradigm, my solution was to disconnect myself from power altogether. I didn't want to be like 'them', so I silenced myself and kept myself small. Now I'm able to recognise that it is exactly our radiance: our creative, intuitive, and compassionate availability and love for all life as leaders that keeps us in sacred relationships with our land, each other, and the planet. The desire to collaborate and compassionately connect rather than conquer and compete is not only our true power, but also critical for our survival as a human race.

On a microcosmic level, we witness how that 'power over' archetype can play out in our individual upbringings and the devastating effect it can have.

Perhaps you grew up in an environment where it simply wasn't safe to be seen or heard. Creating a socially acceptable 'false self' or adopting the role of the 'people pleaser' isn't just the need to be liked—it's a full blown trauma response to keep us safe and alive. When a caregiver threatened to explode into rage, gave us the silent treatment, withdrew their attention, or failed to mirror our vital inner life, it felt like abandonment—death in the mind of a child. Some of us had our nervous systems hardwired to keep our mouths shut from an early age.

The veils that Rumi talks of are the insecurity, self-doubt, fear, anxiety, guilt, and anger of the controlling personality that cover up the radiant light of our authentic being.

CREATING SAFETY

It always starts here. We need to feel safe to know ourselves, safe to see ourselves, and finally, safe to share ourselves.

One day I was sitting in a silent retreat on the stone floor of a temple space in Mexico. Bright pink bougainvillea danced outside the window, while the warmth of the sun and gentle murmur of the sea brought an incredible feeling of peace and beauty. 'This is it!' I thought, 'I'm going to dissolve into nothingness!'

All of a sudden, an agonising cry leapt from the core of my being.

It was the voice of my inner child, that vibrant emotional younger part of me. To her—dissolving into bliss felt like abandonment. That wasn't what she needed right then, and that certainly wasn't what love was about. This younger part wanted to feel seen, heard, and protected.

So much of our visibility journey is reconnecting to that innocent self inside and saying, '*I SEE YOU,*' and '*IT IS GOOD*'.

We need to come home to the safety of our body and find the empowered adult within that no longer acts out of fear-based responses and says firmly, 'I'll take care of you now'.

BOUNDARY BASICS

One of the excruciatingly painful things about enduring disrespectful environments is that it becomes 'the water we swim in'. We become tolerant to poor behaviour simply because it's all we've ever known.

Look at the people around you and in your circle now, answer the following questions, and then take action to help yourself feel safe:

- Who amplifies the best things you think about yourself?
- And conversely who amplifies your insecurities?
- How healthy is your home environment?
- How safe do you feel to share creatively at work?
- How does your home space nurture you?
- Which places feel uplifting?
- Which events or people drain and exhaust you?

And if so—how much access do you give them to your life?

It's essential that we learn how to become a loving parent to ourselves, protect ourselves and our work, self-regulate our emotions, and gain self-acceptance. We all yearn to feel comfortable in our own skin and authentically confident.

For some of us, simply the art of labelling our feelings as they arise and recognizing they are connected to our needs is a novelty. Journal on the following when you feel upset.

- What am I feeling?
- What physical sensations does that create in my body?
- Did something happen or did I do something to make myself feel this way?
- What am I telling myself is true about myself or my life if I believe these thoughts?
- What need is this feeling connected to and what action could I take right now to help myself feel better?

Then please take the action necessary to prove to yourself you're worth caring about!

FINDING OUR EMPOWERED ADULT

I was staying in an inn run by a lovely Tibetan woman in Yunnan Province, China. There was a donkey in the courtyard and red chrysanthemums dotted the hillside. Breakfast was a cup of strong Tibetan coffee and fried baba—a roundel of home made bread smeared in honey and covered in fresh walnuts. I was just about to complete the 14 mile, two day trek, Tiger Leaping Gorge.

When I think back to that strong, courageous woman that chose to do a hike in rural China by herself, that strode across waterfalls and navigated perilously thin mountain paths, I feel calm, and confident. I know that anything is possible, and that I can trust myself and tackle hard things. My chest is open and expansive and my breathing deep and slow. Using this memory, I'm able to invoke this version of a resourced empowered woman. I inhabit her to become the inner parent and offer the sage advice to myself as a good parent or coach would.

What is your empowered memory?

Bring it to life by recalling the physical sensations in your body, your breathing, and your energy. What scents and images come to mind? What feelings? How does this help you tackle life and what do you believe about yourself? Create a vivid visualisation that you can recall at any time.

HER

Owning our Radiant Visibility is a demonstration of unconditional self love, proving to ourselves and the world that we know ourselves, we see ourselves, and yes—what we have to offer is worth shouting about! But many of us struggle with the notion of feeling unconditional love because we've simply never experienced it. Perhaps we can learn to source that experience from a different place.

I was in a small stone room kneeling at a pew. A sense of bewilderment and grief engulfed me. Here in the soft, dark space of this tiny house with archway entrances and a simple altar, I started to cry. My heart gave up her tears and all of my pain rose up to the surface to be washed away. I continued to pray as I could hear tourists shuffle in and out of the space. Gradually, I felt myself cocooned in what I can only describe as a glowing and warm womb space. I was being held in an unconditionally loving energy as if by the tenderest of mothers. I was at the Virgin Mary's house in Ephesus, Turkey.

I stayed until the tears subsided. My contemplation was interrupted by a heavy waft of incense as a Catholic Priest in emerald green strode passed. I was confused—what was he doing here? It took a moment to recollect. My first experience of Her was so utterly beyond any one religion. I had been touched and held by the deepest softest heart of the Divine Feminine.

The blueprint of archetypal energies of the Divine Mother as found in Goddess mythology across spiritual traditions and the sacred Mother energy of nature herself are also, I discovered, able to provide that sense of unconditional love and healing energy.

When we sit in sacred silence with the land, our nervous system naturally entrains to her resonance. Our busy minds relax and drift from beta (everyday) brain waves down into alpha. A rhythm of harmony, creative flow, and deep relaxation envelopes us. As we slow down and rest in stillness, we begin to open in self trust and a trust in life. From this place, our creativity and our intuition can flourish.

But to fully share our gifts, we first need to reconnect with the purity of our deepest desires.

RECONNECTING TO OUR DESIRES

There is no more fitting mythical tale than the one that heralds from these very shores of Northern Scotland. The Selkie is a beautiful seal woman kidnapped by her human husband who has stolen her sealskin and forced her to live on the land. Finally, after seven long years, dried up and with lips cracked, skin blistered and life force almost depleted, she finds her oily skin. Watched by her young son, she slips down to the water's edge and disappears forever beneath the silky waves.

It's a haunting metaphor of a woman who—denied access to her true, wild, and creative self, becomes parched and struggling for life. And it is a warning to all those of us who may have lost their sealskin long ago, buried under mounds of paperwork or nappies, or emails and to-do lists. That is, those who found themselves disconnected from their true calling and stuck on the hamster wheel of perfectionism headed towards burnout and living a notion of success defined by other people.

We may be terrified to listen to that still, small voice within that whispers, 'How did I get here? And what do I truly want anyway?'

Beneath the shiny wrappers of superficial desires—the shopping spree or the bottle of wine—is Desire with a capital D. It is our very lifeforce and begs to be followed with infinite curiosity and awe. This is the vitality that lives at the core of our being. It is the energy that bursts life into the blossom buds, forces the groundswell of the ocean, and sends the sun to drench the earth. Desire is the energy that creates the whole of the glorious world, allowing it to pulse and open in its ever shifting state of expansion.

This Desire has a divine blueprint for our fullest creative expression, too. We are bursting with potential, like the idea of a magnificent oak tree that lives inside its acorn, and the idea of the rose that lives inside her bud.

Spend some time journaling each morning with the question: Deep down in my heart, what do I truly, deeply want?

Do it everyday and write until you run out of things to say. Do it as if your life depends upon it. Because it does.

CONSCIOUSLY CHOOSING OUR LIGHT

In a world rife with political protests, natural disasters, and fake social media news, there is no more critical capacity than to shed the outer influences of societal approval, expectations, and influence and anchor in the wisdom of our hearts.

We follow this path by creating safety in our nervous system, resting in sacred stillness and following the wild Selkie call of our soul. Allowing our radiance to shine isn't just resting in a post-meditative glow, but to completely accept the rawness of our human life and love it unconditionally. When we allow our life force to flow through us, we are present, available to the moment, and able to respond fluidly to whatever arises. We follow the nudges of our intuition and shift into the slipstream of the present moment and the Divine Love that lives both within and outside of us. In complete integrity with our inner life and purpose, we share from our heart naturally and spontaneously from a place of delightful innocence and joy.

The magnetic glow of our inner pearl of radiance draws people to us and reflects the truth—the Love that they are, back to them. In the radiance of Love's light, we lead ourselves and each other home, and in doing so, we ease into that magnificent jigsaw puzzle of life —complete and contributing our part to an ever-expanding whole for the benefit of all beings.

ABOUT THE AUTHOR

DOMINIQUE DIDINAL

Dominique Didinal is the Founder of Radiant Woman™. She helps heart-centered high performers who yearn to make an impact in the world - banish burnout and self sabotage, overcome their fear of being visible and reclaim their authentic confidence to rise to their next level of divine success.

Her Radiant Power™ system works at a rapid, transformative level, not just reprogramming the mind from limiting beliefs, but healing the emotional wounds of the heart that block true radiance. Sacred meditation, embodiment practice, Goddess initiation and coaching, help clients reconnect to their feminine power and intuition and discover deep meaning, joy and legacy for their lives.

A former actress, Brand Strategist and passionate mental health advocate from London, Dominique left behind a successful corporate career to travel the world. She lives in Scotland close to white sandy beaches and the mountains of the Highlands and loves connecting to nature, belly dancing and poetry.

Business Name: Radiant Woman™
Website URL: www.radiant-woman.org
Facebook group: ARadiantWoman
Email: hello@radiant-woman.org

DR. RACHEL KAPUSTKA, CHIROPRACTOR

TRANSCENDENCE

The human body is miraculous. I have had frequent conversations with people around how long a person can live on their deathbed despite debilitating chronic disease. Living this way is not necessarily a high quality of life. Yet, it is jaw-dropping how resilient the body can be even when we may be ready to make our transition spiritually from this realm. I have found it interesting to observe myself and the world putting our faith and inner peace on the "outside in" treatments and approaches to health challenges or perceived external threats. What makes us different as individuals in our abilities and choices? What makes a living person different from a corpse? What makes one person able to adapt and express health where someone else may die as a result of an exposure to a virus or bacteria? In chiropractic, we have a philosophical principle #24 The Limits of Adaptation that states, "Innate Intelligence adapts forces and matter for the body as long as it can do so without breaking a universal law, or Innate Intelligence is limited by the limitations of matter". I also have found limitations to my consciousness impacts the ability of the physical body to functionally adapt thereby limiting the expression of our unique essence. I have experienced that limitations to matter and consciousness impact each other. Our souls, however, are limitless.

As a child, I kind of loved to be tickled. The sensation would make me laugh, which is a valued expression for me, but then the feeling would become intolerable, and I could find myself feeling frustrated or even angry. "Stop, stop, stop", I would yell, but after a few minutes of recovery, I was tempting the tickle fate again. This is an interesting metaphor of how our beings are continually searching for the edges of our life experience and searching for the balance or homeostasis within the body and life. What feels balanced and homeostatic to one can be vastly different from another. My essence is willing to explore a lot, and as a result, I have developed a great expansion and great contraction of my boundaries—the pulse of life.

Physical, mental, and emotional stress can become locked into our neurology at any stage or age in life, yet we know that the most impactful stage is birth through five years old. A baby conceived in love compared to a baby conceived in a traumatic experience will have a different cellular makeup and neurological flexibility. Being a chiropractor who works with pregnant women, I would say that trauma can begin being locked in while we are in the womb. As developing fetuses, we are imprinting mom's neurology and immune system as our own. Is she under physical, emotional, or chemical stress, is she experiencing dis-ease from being locked in a trauma from her childhood, is she in a safe and supportive environment, is she healthy and well-adapted? And what of the birth process? This is where most humans experience their first physical trauma. The length and intensity of labor, a baby being born by use of a vacuum, forceps, or a c-section are all very traumatic to the critical area of the upper cervical spine, which protects the physiological regulatory centers in the brain stem. Our culture tends to be relieved and thankful that the baby has ten fingers and toes, and we never think to have their spine and nerve systems checked by a qualified chiropractor. I often wonder and wish what could have been had a chiropractor checked me when I was a baby. Most people have been living with trauma locked in their neurology for 30, 40, 50, or more years by the time we see them. I was loved and lucky enough to have my spine checked when I was thirteen years old.

I have been through a fair share of challenges this time around on earth. I am the youngest of five girls with a paranoid schizophrenic mother and an alcoholic father. Of course, my parents are so much more than these labels. I have a story based on perceptions and memories of how the lack of adaptive forces in their beings impacted my life. My mother was in a mental institution when she was six months pregnant with me, and the illness prevented her from properly caring for my sisters and I. My father was advised by a judge to take us girls before we ended up in foster care. My Dad did take us, and as such is my hero. I have no doubt that our home was full of love and it was also full of challenges. These family experiences may have contributed to the potential of my body to express disease. I remember as a child feeling scared, unsure of myself and my surroundings. I was home alone a lot around the ages of 4 and 5 years old and too young to understand why or understand the impact until I was an adult. Everyone was doing their best to survive with the tools they had in hand. I understand this as an adult but did not as a child. There are so many stories that allowed me to define myself from these years of survival. When I was around nineteen years old I saw a therapist who helped me see how the loss and aloneness taught me responsibility. The ability to respond to life. I developed many coping strategies. Some of my strategies were effective and some came with life long consequences.

I engaged in alcohol and sexual activity at a young age. I was looking to feel something other than sorrow and searching for love in all the wrong ways and wrong places. I married young, and he had what I perceived to be a stable family, yet the hole in my heart stayed open and hidden. I divorced young, married and divorced again, and then married another time (third time's a charm). I was a dysfunctional type A person. I worked several jobs at once, went to school full time, and made straight A's. I would go days without sleeping, I would exercise up to 4 hours a day, fueled myself on low fat, high sugar foods, or I would not eat at all, and of course, no protein because I learned that was bad for the planet. I was malnourished and suffered from occasional seizures. I was terrified to be alone. Who would I be if I were not living with or for someone else? I was a girl who went from relationship to relationship like I was playing on the monkey bars in the school yard.

I was diagnosed with Type 1 diabetes in my early 20's and then kidney failure in my 40's. I have judged and criticized myself as being weak, unworthy of love, high maintenance, and a burden to others for needing medicine, dialysis, and someone else's kidney to survive. I have blamed, shamed and chosen to be a victim of circumstance. Every day requires energy, attention, action, and commitment to not only stay alive but also to feel alive. I make mistakes all of the time. I forget to take my medicine or forget to pack my insulin and immunosuppressant drugs on a trip. I prioritize someone else when I should be prioritizing myself. Not taking care of me first comes at a high price for everyone. I have been near death five times from diabetic hypoglycemia, diabetic ketoacidosis, and kidney infections. Sometimes I take too much medicine, or my equipment fails, which severely dysregulates my body. The recovery takes days and sometimes weeks from these episodes. I need to move when all I want to do is rest. I need to eat when I'm not hungry. I need to dose insulin when I haven't had anything to eat. I need to monitor and manage my stress levels when all I want to do is lose my mind or put my head in the sand. Everything impacts everything.

I have always known I wanted babies. When my husband and I started dating, we would talk about having ten kids. We were drunk on love and life. We were pregnant a couple of times and miscarried a couple of times until we finally gave birth to our magicman. He was 11 months old when we had his hearing tested. We were grateful that he wasn't screened at birth so we could just enjoy falling in love with him. When he was around four months old, my husband noticed he wasn't responding to sound. I didn't see it because I held him, wore him, or slept with him all of the time. Sure enough, on a Thursday, we got the news that he had bilateral profound hearing loss. I think we were both in shock. We never considered this as a possibility. I didn't realize how many assumed expectations there were inside of me about how I would mother. I imagined reading books aloud, anticipated what his voice would sound like, I was excited to document his first spoken words, I wondered what songs we would sing together, and dreamed of being dancing fools in the kitchen. The visions of parenthood flashed like flipping polaroid photos through my mind and disappeared into thin air without any image, dream, vision, or anticipation to replace all that I thought would be. What a gift that keeps on giving. The next day, we found a basic sign language manual on our shelf. We headed to a coffee shop while our son napped in his car seat next to us and memorized the 200 hundred signs in the book. We met with local specialists, which led to ASL classes, trips to meet with surgeons to learn about cochlear implants, met families who chose the surgical path, we watched documentaries about the Deaf, we started running into Deaf people everywhere we went, we traveled to meet Deaf people, we went to ASL immersion camps, listened to panels of young Deaf people talking about growing up in hearing families and schools with only the ASL interpreter to communicate through, we would visit Deaf schools for our spring breaks to see if we needed to move in order to provide the best education for our son.

We found a common story of inhumanity. We found young people with a weak self-identity, often no relationship with their families, developmental delays because of language barriers, and it was heartbreaking. We were determined that the stories we heard would not be our son's experiences. If we went anywhere and saw someone signing, we immediately introduced ourselves, told our story, and people were open-armed and willing to support our journey. We made sure we had items labeled with English words throughout the house, that we signed as much as we could with the signs we knew. We had closed captioning on the television, we advocated for appropriately licensed and skilled interpreters in school, and we had signing videos playing in the background as much as possible for our whole family's learning. When our son was five years old, we made a move. We could no longer tolerate the inadequacy of support in our school system. We found a small charter school for the Deaf. Everyone at the school uses ASL all of the time, and our son would have direct access to his peers and teachers. We sold our home and business and left our wonderful lifestyle, yet we needed and wanted more support than what was available where we lived. We found it, and sighed with relief. All of the sacrifice to have this support would be worth it, but the relief was short-lived. We were in our new home and our new business for only a few months when I had blood work drawn to establish my new healthcare practitioner. He shared the grim news that my kidneys were only functioning at 6%, and I needed to see a nephrologist immediately.

When the kidney failure diagnosis came, I sank to the bottom of the barrel. I was exhausted from the daily grind of managing my health, motherhood, being a wife and being a doctor, grieving, leaving our home, and trying to get a new business going. I considered the option of non-treatment which meant living out however many days I had left until my heart stopped. I scheduled the surgery for peritoneal dialysis, but I wasn't convinced it's what I wanted to do. Every day, I went through the motions, but I was mentally, emotionally, and physically disengaged. I was under a rock. One night, my husband and I were watching a movie where a mother had to abandon her child. The scene triggered my old abandonment wounds and sparked an anxiety attack out of this world. The pain that I tapped into made me convulse with tears. I sat up as I panicked, trying to rip off my clothes. My mind wanted me to run as if I could escape the horrendous feeling of pain, gasping for air and no place to go. I wanted to die at that moment; I wanted to feel peace. The experience felt like an eternity as I rode the tidal wave of fear. As the exhaustion set in, my heart calmed, and my breathing slowed, I became clear with this divine intervention. I must choose life for my son. I must not leave him or my husband. I need to do whatever it takes to stay alive for as long as possible for them, I thought. They became my driving force for survival.

Dialysis was hell. I was thankful to do the exchanges at home, and the process was grueling and painful. The hoops one has to jump through to be listed for an organ transplant is also grueling. Every week I jumped through a hoop, and every day I did my best to take care of myself. Once I was listed, we learned it's an average of 5 years to receive a kidney. I didn't know how I could do dialysis for this long, and luckily, I didn't have to find out. A practitioner I was working with told me that his mail lady was donating her kidney. I listened yet said nothing. Later I shared the story with my husband, who asked if I gave him permission to share my contact information. I was overcome with my absent-mindedness! I immediately texted my practitioner, gave him permission, and ten minutes later, he was introducing us to each other over a text message. I could have dropped to the floor with cautious optimism. We talked over the phone the next day, and she teased me about my first question to her. "What is your blood type", I asked. There was no point in continuing the conversation if we didn't at least have the same kind of blood. We have the same blood type, as well as other important factors and five months later, we were in the hospital together to transplant her kidney into my body. Truly miraculous, generous, and life giving of this complete stranger and is now a sister from a different mother to me.

I thought this life-saving procedure would be my new lease on life. I believed I would come out of surgery so inspired and hopeful to live my best life. I would prove that I was worth this organ, and I would do it for my donor, for the doctors, anyone going through something similar and for my family. Instead, I went into a very deep depression. I'm sure it was a combination of all that led up to the procedure, the surgery itself, the pain, the medication, and all the darkness I had yet to realize lurking in the background. I felt tremendous guilt and shame that I was depressed and that I was contemplating suicide. I wouldn't get out of bed for days at a time. During this stage of healing, what was helpful to me were the people who held space for this dark side of me. They didn't act out of fear or make me feel wrong. They just loved me through. They allowed me to be in this place without judgment.

I have come in and out of this depression as I believe what can be more readily tapped into is old pain, old stories, old perceptions, and old sadness stored in my neurology. What has kept me going is the joy of watching my son grow, holding him when he is sad or hurt, laughing with him, being silly with me, doing funny dances in the kitchen, watching him kill it on the soccer field, witnessing his drive and effort to be his best and his sense of humor. As my body has become stronger, my inherent desire to be curious and discover myself has allowed one day to lead into another. I celebrate every year on my transplant anniversary with my donor, and her zest for life is a blessing to be around and have in my body. What also keeps me going is my husband and our journey as partners on this planet and my ambition to get our connection stronger and deeper. I surround myself with amazing humans and lightworkers who are willing to have big deep talks. I do yoga every day to connect to my divinity and connect to my breath. I get chiropractic care, bodywork and acupuncture regularly. I eat well, take my supplements and move my body. I talk to my loved ones and I'm authentic with where I am. I do my best to stay in the eye of the storm, put my faith in the divine spirit inside of me, keep my heart open, and celebrate often. I touch people, and I allow my body to be a conduit for others' healing. I love them and hold space for them as others have done for me, and most importantly, I have added myself to the list of reasons to live. When I live for myself, I am living for God, and I am better able to serve others, including my son, my husband, my family and the people I serve.

My search for the why's and the how's of my path has led me on an amazing journey of self-discovery. At times, I wanted to give up. Yet, the drive to understand the meaning of my path has led me to become a doctor that is filled with empathy and compassion, a woman who cherishes life and the simple joys that come in a fleeting moment, a mother of a brilliant Deaf son who is my greatest teacher, a wife to my devoted and equally wounded warrior husband, a thankful daughter, a loving sister and a hell of a fun friend. The ability to be courageous, truthful, sincere, and responsible for my feelings and actions with my patients and myself has developed over time and with what feels like an eternity of self-introspection. I have found humor in the gravest of scenarios in my personal experiences and those of our patients to be transcendent. What also has moved me beyond the pain and sorrow is gratitude. I am thankful for all of the good things that have and continue to happen in my life, and I take the time to express my appreciation of the events, the wisdom, and the people who are integral in the weaving of my life story. One might judge that enough is enough, yet for me, I value curiosity. I take an interest in ongoing encounters with being a human on this earth. I am fascinated by a variety of subjects and topics in order to explore and discover more about who I am and the meaning of life. The juice has been in the depths of my darkness, and mostly it's been about love. When I have been shown love when I'm living in my shadow or at the bottom of the barrel is what is most beautiful. In those moments, I'm reminded that I am worthy and I am enough. It's about humanity. It's about valuing my relationship with myself and others, especially where there is an exchange of sharing and caring. I value connection and being close to people, like two molecules under a microscope magnetizing to each other to become something else, to collaborate and create something greater and simply to just be.

My soul mission is to understand your heart and for you to understand mine. Empathy is one of my favorite ASL signs. The visual communication is made by touching your heart with your middle finger then simultaneously flicking both pointer fingers upward. One pointer finger represents the person in front of you while the other represents you. When I sign "empathy" to you, I am saying that my heart understands your heart. When our hearts understand each other, we move beyond to a greater quality of love, acceptance of what is, a greater depth of understanding and independence of fear, worry, selfishness, anger, greed, jealousy, hate, and anything else we might judge as a negative or unpleasant emotion. Love is the language that elicits change leading to triumph over the negative and restrictive aspects we can encounter on this planet. Dive into the deep end, where you will find the shadows of your soul's existence and embrace the nutrients that thrive in this place for your growth and evolution as a human being on this earth. Put your trust in yourself, your body, and the divine within. To gain clarity of my purpose and mission as a soul, this is where I have needed to spend more time. In the darkness. Understand what you value, take inventory of your trauma, and find gratitude for the gifts and blessings that come in the form of joy and sorrow, pleasure and pain. Many of us judge that the more pain we have been through, the more broken we are and undeserving of love. My dearest friend and I have a saying. More plus more equals more. The more we are willing to encounter, the more love and wisdom we bring to ourselves and then to others. May you have the courage to shine light in your darkest corners. May you be loved, be love and give love to the judgments that hide in that darkness. May you see, feel, honor and embrace all of you. May you shine your light on this earth.

ABOUT THE AUTHOR

DR. RACHEL KAPUSTKA

Dr. Rachel Kapustka is the owner and practitioner at Realm Chiropractic in Lakewood, CO and Live Ketostyle. She provides functional corrective care which allows clients to live and express themselves more fully while increasing their adaptability to life. Dr. Rachel's skills as a chiropractor and a keto lifestyle coach supports healing on a cellular level creating better ways for people to live while being held in a safe place for growth mentally, emotionally, physically and spiritually.

Dr. Rachel resides in Colorado with her husband, son and their bulldog, Mojo. She loves connecting with the community, family, friends and being in nature, pursuing yoga certifications and being a soccer mom.

Email: Drrkapustka@gmail.com
*Website:*www.realmlakewood.com
Facebook: https://www.facebook.com/ketostylelive
https://www.facebook.com/realmlakewood

TINA D'AMORE

VOICES OF THE SPIRITS

"Mankind is notoriously too dense to read the signs that God sends from time to time. We require drums to be beaten into our ears, before we should wake from our trance and hear the warning and see that to lose oneself in all, is the only way to find oneself."

~ Mahatma Gandhi

The practice of shamanism has shaped me into who I am today, and is currently shaping me into who I will become tomorrow. In fact, I didn't know what shamanism really was when I was pulled onto this path by the spirits. I merely entered into the shamanic worlds with a personal hope that it could save my life. I am in deep gratitude to be one of the many living testaments to the power of shamanism, as I wouldn't be physically alive without this ancient, sacred practice. As terribly challenging as my personal story onto the shamanic path may have been, I find myself extraordinarily lucky to have benefited from the rebirthing that historically describes the shamanic initiation: the process of "becoming" a shaman.

Shamanism is the most ancient spiritual practice known to humankind. Many anthropologists believe that the practice dates back 100,000 years. Shamanism has been practiced in Asia, Europe, Africa, Australia, North America and South America. Rooted in the language of the Tungus people of Siberia, the word *shaman* translates to "one who sees in the dark" or "one who knows." A shaman is a woman or man who uses the capacity to see with "a strong eye" or "strong heart" to travel into the shamanic worlds with the intention of partnering with specific, divine beings called Helping Spirits.

How does one become a shamanic practitioner? The spirits choose the shaman. There are many stories of shamans whose initiatory experience consisted of overcoming severe illness, living after being struck by lightning, being born with a caul, having Near-Death Experiences, having seizures, and incurring insufferable traumas impacting the spiritual, mental, emotional, and physical levels of the shaman-to-be. However, it was not only the challenges the neophyte endured, but how he or she transmuted sickness of any form into effective medicine for the community. Not only would the neophyte need to be metaphorically born again into this world, but he or she must also show the capacity to work effectively with his or her Helping Spirits to provide service to the community. To this day, it is in the effectiveness with which the practitioner communes with one's Helping Spirits in the transcendental realms to bring back information and healing into this world, that the community then recognizes the shaman.

Historically, the shaman not only heard the voices of the spirits, but she also *became* the spirits. Her skin would become vacant of her bones and she would house her Helping Spirits in her body. Her words would slice through illusion and see the heart of a person, an animal or tree, a situation in question, and the Heart of Mother Earth. All of this was due to the embodiment of her Helping Spirits. It is from this place she would create great change within, which would ripple out to create great change externally.

In December 2007, my own initiation commenced at the age of 34 as I began to experience severe symptoms of a mysterious illness. At that point, I had become incapacitated with horrendous daily body pain, memory loss, processing issues, disorientation, dyspnea, incapacitating migraines, insomnia lasting for months, alarming lymph node swelling, tremors, ataxia, dyskinesia, seizures, as well as another neurological condition called generalized dystonia.

By early 2008, I found myself in a wheelchair and living with my parents and now late grandfather on the coast of Maine. I had already lost my job, my apartment, some friends, a boyfriend, and my retirement savings. Most importantly, I had lost my health and what I thought was my identity as an educator in grades K-3.

By the end of 2010, I had seen over 25 doctors in Maine and in the Boston area. No one could tell me what was happening. In fact, some of the top neurologists in New England even told me that there was nothing wrong with me at all - and worse - coldly stated that my mind was "playing tricks" on me. Even after the diagnosis of Lyme disease and several co-infections in 2011, as well as the following years of intense treatment, I didn't know if the moment-to-moment pain and misery would ever end. The treatment made the symptoms even more intense. Some days did not find me feeding, bathing, or clothing myself. I even lost the ability to coherently speak at times.

By late 2013, I had a secret bottle of hydrocodone in my nightstand, just in case. It was more of a thought of comfort than a desire: the comfort of escaping if I just couldn't take it any longer. Even if I did live, I didn't know if I was going to spend the rest of my days as a burden to every person in my life. It seemed my existence had become filled by nothing but medical equipment and caretakers.

I have a friend of over 20 years who would visit me weekly. Recently she confided in me that each time she left, she wasn't sure she'd ever see me again. I never told her that each time she left, I didn't know if I'd make it to her next weekly visit. My parents later divulged that they had thought the same.

There were times that I would be deeply comforted to share the days' most intimate moments involving a sugar maple outside my bedroom window. I still recall the world stopping with the incoming of gentle spring air and maple flower buds; the passing of time with the summer cicadas' humming amongst the denser wind and the rich verdant leaves that had unfolded; the scampering of gray squirrels through autumn's magnificent gold, coral and crimson leaves; and the quiet Maine snow blanketing the bareness of the branches. When I moved from that house years later, I sobbed, acknowledging that I made it out alive. I also sobbed saying goodbye to that beautiful tree and the compassionate nature spirits of the land who walked with me for that time.

Making sense of several Near-Death Experiences has been one of the most challenging parts of my recovery. It is often expressed by NDE'ers that coming back to one's body with new perceptions of the universe without anyone around to truly understand those perceptions can be daunting. NDE's seem to blow normal circuitry in the brain, so drastic change occurs with one's state of mind, perceptions and also how the NDE'er embodies the experience. In a world of the mundane, having directly experienced the vibration of Oneness can be a lonely path in this human world. It's as if there is a sacred secret ready to burst forth but no one is capable of empirically understanding. The level of compassion and interconnectedness that is contained in the heart and spirit from such an otherworldly experience is sometimes met with misunderstanding and rejection from those who only draw experience of one mundane reality. Living in forgetfulness is not truly living at all. Shamans of old have understood that this realm is a collective dream, one that we have the power to influence and change for the worse or for the better.

One of my NDE's occurred during a severe dystonic episode. At this point in my treatment, I had been to the small town emergency room too many times. We had lost hope that they would try to understand that these were not seizures and that I was not seeking attention or a high from prescribed substances. My diaphragm had locked up and, from what I've been told by my parents who witnessed my physical experience, I could inhale only slightly every 15-20 seconds. I recall my muscles relentlessly contracting and contorting me like an invisible boa constrictor. I was in one position for two hours as the medications, dosed three times, were not effective in stopping the episode. I could hear everything being said but I could not get my mouth or tongue to move in order to speak words. In fact, I could barely make a sound other than slight moaning powered only by weak breath. Gradually, my line of sight blackened and I felt my thoughts dissolve and my spirit drift off above my body.

I suddenly found myself in a plane of the cosmos in a cloudy landscape in a dimension I did not recognize. I could not see more than gray clouds but I heard my Helping Spirits quite clearly. There seemed to be an entire team speaking lovingly to me but with a sense of urgency. "Claim yourself! Hold your ground and ignite the power of the universe within you! It is trying to take you!"

My attention focused on a large thing approaching me through the gray landscape, focusing its flight intently on me. It was covered in olive scales and was carried by immense wings adorned in skin. If it had appeared in this world, it would have been the size of a bus. Filled with fear, I wanted to crawl up inside myself while simultaneously feeling it drawing out my life force, weakening me. "Claim who you are!" I heard familiar voices. As I pulled back my life force, I felt this lightning bolt of energy run through me, expanding me, until I was as big as the dragon.

I declared, "This is my spirit, and that is my body! I am part of everything. I AM that I AM!" I stood my ground while looking into its eyes, which were hauntingly familiar. I saw beneath its intent to take me, to the fear and sadness behind its eyes. In the next moment, the creature pulled away from me as if caught in an invisible tornado. Concerned, I asked my Helping Spirits to bring this being to a dimension that was compassionate, aligning it with a level of consciousness for its Highest Good. I trust this being is now part of the Oneness we all are derived from.

After this, I seemed to fall through time, crashing back into my physical body and gasping for breath. Utterly exhausted, my parents moved me from the floor to the couch so I could recover. The experience seemed like an entire day. Being so surreal, it took me weeks to understand what had occurred. To this day, it seems like a dream.

Another afternoon had already brought two painful and terrifying dystonic episodes which started with a transient seizure. I lay on my bed like a wild broken mustang, staring at the ceiling. I had decorated the area of the ceiling over my bed with selected calendar prints of Georgia O'Keeffe's inspiring work. I silently asked Georgia, my Helping Spirits, and God, *Show me how I might live through this.*

Already dissociated from the intense pain and the fogginess of my thinking mind from the neurological activity, I began to journey into the spiritual dimension of this realm without the use of traditional sound. I began to hear the divine whispers of my Helping Spirits as if they were physical beings in my bedroom. They told me that it no longer mattered that I had taught young children in school, what my dreams were to keep walking that path, what my ancestry was, what my personal likes and dislikes were, what my name was, or even my gender.

I asked, *What does matter, then?*

I was shown a Divine Golden Seed. It moved closer towards my waking eyes and grew bigger with a message of great importance. As the seed was brought into my body, I was told to do everything I could to nurture, water, and care for the seed so it could grow. I was told to surrender everything else. I heard their ancient, sacred whispers and messages, of which I cannot share. I glanced at the sugar maple outside and began to understand.

I had to let go of everything: the utter misery of my daily life, the illusion of my illness and who I thought I was. I came to understand that I needed to accept my life in the present: the wheelchair, the bedside commode, and the caretaker who made daily visits. I had to

balance that acceptance with focus in manifesting what I truly
desired. I realized this focus had to contain my unwavering act of
filling myself with life force. Although this seemed impossible to do
given that everything around me reflected back that I would stay
completely dependent on others for the rest of my days, or possibly
even die, I chose to feed my new life. I began practicing an esoteric
healing technique called Transfiguration, or Healing with Light,
while envisioning myself returning to complete wellness. When I
practiced daily, I could feel myself slowly being lifted out of the
vibration of the illness. It wasn't over yet, though.

In another Near-Death Experience, I was met by an angelic being
and was shown the Light. He said, "You are suffering a lot. We
know you are in much pain. If you wish, you may let go of your
body and come Home where there is no more suffering. The choice
is yours and there is no judgment in whatever you choose." I saw the
Light. It was absolutely beautiful and welcoming. I felt such peace
and an immense sense of belonging.

I looked back at my body, my mother yelling over me, "Tina! Tina!!
BREATHE!!!" I was lying in the middle of the kitchen floor where I
had collapsed, now gasping for air during yet another dystonic
episode. I had been feeling out of it most of the day, disoriented and
fuzzy, my body weak and tremoring. I knew it was coming, but I
never knew quite when.

I thought hard about it for a moment: *It certainly would be nice to not
suffer daily like this anymore.* But to my surprise, words flew out of me,
yelling into the vast expanse of where my spirit was with the angelic
being, "No! I have too much to do!" Immediately, I slammed back
into my body, gasped for air and was welcomed back by the
unrelenting pain.

My own words echoed from the realm I returned from. *I have too
much to do?* But what exactly did that mean? I began to choose to live
as I was being asked: to let these compassionate spirits speak their
words through me. I chose to crack open to let go of the notion of

who I perceived I was and I surrendered to the unfolding. I hung onto the vision of the Golden Seed, grasped onto it like it was my lifeline, because it was. The "sick" me seemed to slowly disintegrate into oblivion. All of what I endured would begin to have even more meaning as I began to pay it forward to others in serving my community. I have hung onto the feeling, the potential, the hope, and the vibration of that Seed and will continue to do so until I finally return back Home.

No one can be truly at the point of surrender until they are willing to let go of identifying with one's own dis-ease, whatever their obstacles to wellness are. For those with chronic illness, this is tricky because in letting go of that identification, one has to let go of the diagnosis. Letting go of the need to be validated by a medical professional creates a huge shift. In truly wanting to be well, giving power to the illness is counterproductive. Attributing every symptom to the illness is feeding it, and when this happens we keep ourselves in a small box and give our power away. We are more than we think we are!

Feeling the will to heal deep in the bones, while also acknowledging any victim-consciousness within is a big step to shift the relationship to the illness. Read this with an open heart: the dis-ease is not happening to you, it is happening *for* you, despite how symptoms might feel at times or how it has changed life in any perceived negative way. What is the illness teaching that hasn't been acknowledged? Back up from the lens of the usual perspective and observe what the illness is mirroring back. Be curious, honest, and vulnerable. Drop into a sacred space within, just for the glory of Self. Change the perception of the dis-ease to a personal teacher and perceive it as a tough love partner moving you onto a path to a more authentic Self.

Along with surrendering and allowing, power up with self-compassion, self-love, and self-respect by realizing that we are really part of the Divine, no matter what is happening. Just realizing this can shift so much. Imagine cultivating the world like a seed that is ready for germination. What might it look like? How is it growing? Are there undesirable weeds or are there beautiful vines and flowers? What needs to be done to begin cultivating the dream within? We are all part of this divine creation. We have all the power inside to create our lives. The shamans of old knew that we must dream up the world we wish to live in. Whether initiated by the spirits to become a shamanic practitioner or not, we all have the power to create deep change and move through what seems impossible.

In our Western culture, we are disconnected from Self, each other, and the Earth. I can personally say that the experience of having Lyme disease and co-infections distorts reality because connection to Self is already being invalidated by most medical professionals who are not Lyme-literate. Any previous wounding of invalidation is then magnified when experiencing that desperation for answers. The sufferer is then brought to a level of more disconnect and more dissociation from her body. This can occur with any illness. Therefore, a medical professional, who supposedly has the answers but cannot give any, may deflect and project onto the patient if incapable of providing any solid explanation. The symptoms exhibited may have challenged their expertise in the field, inciting an insecurity within themselves. Don't take those projections on. Don't sit in self-doubt simply because doctors are supposed to know. In the ancient practice of shamanism, giving away our power to anything outside of the wisdom of ourselves is linked to how disease can take hold. Listen to the deep wisdom in the body. It knows!

Soul Retrieval is an ancient healing ceremony that was traditionally implemented by the ancestors immediately after a trauma. There was a conscious understanding of the occurrence of soul loss as it happened. In shamanic cultures, it was common knowledge that during a physical or emotional trauma, the spirit would be affected too.

In modern times, many people walking this world inhabit their bodies with significant soul loss because such ancient spiritual knowledge is unfortunately not widely understood today. Soul loss can be a result of physical, emotional and sexual abuse. Soul loss can occur as a result of rape, acts of war, being held captive, domestic violence, car accidents, and early childhood trauma. It can be a result of a divorce or the death of a loved one. Soul loss may have played a part in becoming ill for some and may occur during a severe illness in others. Adding to the loss of power, massive soul loss has the capacity to create more of an opening in the soul in which illness can root itself and take further hold. Soul loss might feel as if "something is missing." This is the language of soul loss. Modern psychologists call this phenomenon "dissociation," but the ancestors in shamanic cultures knew to remedy this as soon as possible. Soul Retrieval requires the intention to bring back the pure Soul Essence(s) that left due to a negative event. The parts of us that left may not know how to find the way back or may not know that it is now safe to come Home. Each Soul Essence, untainted by the negative events that caused the departure, is welcomed Home to resituate itself back in the body and to fill the deep void that once existed. The ceremony of Soul Retrieval creates a sense of wholeness within that can be life-changing.

In this culture, we are stuck in a paradigm of patriarchy so deeply embedded that we keep giving our power away to others who we believe are "more" or "better." But everything we need to know is within. We are so lucky to live in an era where we greatly benefit from Western medicine. For hundreds of thousands of years, our ancestors derived wise medicine from the natural world, but it may have not always saved lives. In modern times, we can benefit from the magic of both worlds and choose accordingly, with our own intuition and our own sovereignty.

However, as a collective, we no longer listen to the whispers of nature, our own intuition, our bodies, or the language of the spirit world. Our culture has grown out of sync with the natural wisdom flowing inside and outside of us. Instead, our culture supports consuming to fill the void within because we have so much soul loss, individually and collectively. Consumerism only serves to distract us momentarily from our suffering. No matter how much we fill that void with TV, food, casual sex, gambling, substances or unneeded material items, we have not truly filled ourselves of anything with substance. Despite how we might try to block out the suffering, it may be unclear in our mind what we truly have use for. But unlike our mind, our heart and spirit can never be tricked into wholeness by meaningless external factors.

One of my favorite sayings by Zen master, Thích Nhất Hạnh, deeply resonates with me: "No mud, no lotus." Imagine that we all have this lotus flower seed within us. What might that seed look like? What is the beauty hidden deep in that seed? Where does it reside within the body? What might that lotus look like in beautiful, fearless bloom? What does it feel like being in its grace? This grace is *you*. Nothing external can tarnish the grace of that seed. Now, imagine your own suffering is the mud you're standing in. This is the mud that feeds your lotus seed within.

So healing isn't about pushing away the mud, denying that the mud is even there, or attempting to convince oneself that the mud isn't as dirty or sticky as it actually is. Authentic healing is about becoming vulnerable, learning to surrender, to allow, to embrace the mud and transmute it. For it is only in the mud that we find the nutrients of growth for the lotus. If we don't acknowledge the mud, we cannot learn how to feed the lotus. If we cannot see the lotus within, it won't be able to germinate. We might not know how that mud could possibly feed that seed, but it is our task to transmute the mud into medicine that will feed it. It has the capacity to grow with radiance and such beautiful power!

It's up to us whether to allow others into our sacred arena who are worthy of supporting us in our quest to find our own Golden Seed within and to feed it while holding ourselves in sacred space as it blooms. We need to find the courage to reach deep within and trust that everything inside is accessible to walk through the impossible fire. We can learn wonderful things about ourselves as we become more comfortable with the uncomfortable. In the sacred state of the truth of who we really are, including all our desires and dreams, *anything is possible*. Feel that power, like a chrysalis of our own rhythm beginning to pulse, promising to break into the external world with new form. Feel the wisdom in the bones: that wisdom is the Ancestors and their dreams for us. Give birth to the concept that *you* are a truly powerful being.

ABOUT THE AUTHOR

TINA D'AMORE

Tina D'Amore is the founder and owner of 3 Crows Healing: Shamanic Medicine & Animal Whispering. A former educator, she works closely with her Helping Spirits to shift the spiritual cause of disease. After overcoming a severe illness that caused multiple Near-Death Experiences, Tina is attuned to the magnificence of the worlds available to us, including the world we share together. She facilitates sessions with the sole intention of empowering her clients' Inner Fire, intuitively creating sacred space to peel away layers of old programming. Tina adores communicating with animals to shift behavioral or health issues and guiding children in honoring and utilizing their intuitive gifts. She also performs Land Ceremony and loves connecting with the Wee Folk.

Tina lives in southern Maine where she welcomes hikes in the woods, yoga, visiting the ocean, writing, creating art and birdwatching.

3 Crows Healing: Shamanic Medicine & Animal Whispering

Website: www.3crowshealing.com
Email: 3crowshealing@gmail.com
Facebook: https://www.facebook.com/3crowshealing

AMANDA SULLIVAN

UNBOIL YOUR FROG

*I*f you're a woman (and it's okay if you're not), somebody, or likely many somebodies, have had *the talk* with you. No, not *that* talk, the talk where you learn that you're essentially prey, and that around every corner, predators lie in wait. We are taught to always beware of our surroundings, be alert, cautious, and prepared to fight or take flight. If you live in a city, run before daylight, get off work after dark, park in a public parking garage, or live in a garden-level apartment, then vigilance has likely become second nature to you. Stories of dark alleys, creepy vans, and handsome strangers asking for help are just some of the cautionary tales that have been passed down from generation to generation and have become crucial to our survival.

Unfortunately, there are much more pervasive threats out there, hiding in plain sight. They are just as sinister and equally deadly, yet they are not paid the same heed or given the same gory lore as the real-life, big, bad wolves lurking out there. These dangers do not jump out at us suddenly. They infiltrate our lives little by little, every day, in every way. They do not appear scary, dangerous, or deceitful. In fact, many of them look, sound, smell, feel, and taste wonderful, heavenly, even magically delicious.

These insidious dangers are in the food we eat, the beverages we drink, the medicines we're prescribed, the water we bathe in, the air we breathe, the soaps we lather, the creams we slather, the cleaning supplies we gather, and so on. In fact, unless you are vigilantly avoiding them as if Jack the Ripper himself were on the prowl, then you're surrounded by them day in and day out, 24/7/365.

If you've never heard it, the premise of the boiling frog parable is this: if you drop old Kermit into a boiling pot, he will realize that he's just found himself in a bit of hot water and do his best to jump out. However, if you put him in tepid water and slowly bring it to a boil, the poor unsuspecting fellow will adapt slowly as the temperature increases. Unaware of the creeping change in his circumstances, he will unwittingly be boiled alive.

I share this metaphor because we are no different than our buddy Kermit. We didn't just hop into a pot of toxic soup one day; we have been stewing in it our entire life. And, thanks to the slow boil, we often do not recognize the slow degeneration in our quality of life. We are so accustomed, that few even know what it feels like not to be toxic and not to be living in a state of dis-ease. Toxicity is a constant din in this day and age, just an app running in the background, largely because we have pawned it off as a million different other things. For some, it has been diagnosed as eczema. For others, it's been labeled ADD/ADHD. Some identify it as Candida or fibromyalgia, and for many, it has been named anxiety and depression. This is because the burden of toxicity manifests differently for different people. Toxicity in my body may present as a gut issue, where in my brother (same DNA), it may express as a skin condition. They may seem like two totally different ailments, but at the root of most degenerative disease and illness is toxicity. Toxins overwhelm and shut down the weakest links in our bodies. And, because they have infiltrated every facet of our lives, toxins are some of the foulest of tricksters, thugs, and thieves.

Yes, it's a dangerous and toxic world we live in, but the point of this chapter is not to freak you out or send you diving headfirst into the sand. I promise that you can keep reading and still maintain your sanity. In fact, I'm here to help you see just how easy it is to start shifting bit by itty-bitty-bit and take back your life from these surreptitious devils in disguise.

So, for those of you saying to yourself, "I know she's prolly right but ain't nobody got time for that rabbit hole she's trying to shove me down," I hear ya. I know you. And, I was you. Believe me, I have chosen bliss over ignorance MANY times to avoid hard work and big changes. So, hear me out on this, what I'm going to tell you is not hard, it is not outrageously expensive (actually, in the long run, it will save you tens if not hundreds of thousands of dollars) and, I am NOT going to tell you that you have to give up your favorite foods, activities, desserts, etc. What I *am* here to help you do is LIVE your life fully, for longer, with more ease and less dis-ease.

Okay, good, now that you're with me on that, I'll drop another unpopular truth; none of us, and I do mean NONE of us, are getting any younger. However, some of us appear to be aging more slowly than others. And that, my friends, is what this Anti/Aging Junkie is all about. I'm not just talking about fewer wrinkles, glowing hair, and a rockin' body (although I do highly recommend you give yourself all of those). I'm talking about a sexy, sharp mind, beautifully balanced hormones, organs that slay all day, mental health to die for, a digestive system that is the S#!T, a nervous system that isn't always making you nervous, etc., etc., etc. All of that and more can be yours, my friend. Seriously!

So, here's the catch, you can't overcomplicate it. We are all too familiar with the hard way to get those things…Hollywood and social media wave hard-won results in our face that came at a cost few of us can or want to afford…deprivation, iron-clad willpower, painstaking diligence, masterful planning, a personal assistant, personal trainer, personal chef, blah, blah, blah, NAH! Sure, you can get it that way…errr, maybe you're not JLo, and you can't. But, you don't have to have those resources to have incredible outcomes.

Here's why—one of, if not THE primary cause of accelerated aging is higher toxic load. I don't care who you are, the best genes in the world can't save you if you bombard your body with toxins. On the other hand, you could draw the genetic short straw, and if you detoxify your lifestyle, you can cheat illness, disease, and death with Hollywood's most hallowed.

To be clear, my mission is not merely to extend the *quantity* of life. After all, who wants to live to be 100 if the last 20 years are fraught with illness and indignity? My mission is to expand and extend the *quality* of life.

I'm also not talking about living a life of deprivation and sacrifice in order to live longer and/or better. Again, the goal for my clients and for me is ultimate quality of life, and for some (myself included), a well-lived life includes ice cream. I don't eat it every night or even every week. And, when I do, I choose the highest quality available, free of growth hormones and toxic chemicals; but I have my ice cream and eat it too.

For me (and for most people I know), sticking to diets and lifestyle choices that prohibit our favorite things equals deprivation, and deprivation typically ends one of two ways: for the iron-willed, they stick to the rules and swear off some of life's simple joys, thus sacrificing the quality of life. For the rest of us, we deny ourselves for a time and then go way overboard when we fall off the proverbial wagon. And that leaves us feeling like big ol' failures. Both endings are pretty sucky, and I'm not much for sucky endings. Instead, I'm a work smarter to play harder kind of girl. For me that means that roughly 90% of my choices are inspired by my passion for health and wellness. The other 10% of my choices are purely for pleasure, but with 0% guilt. In fact, I believe that the whole idea of 'guilty pleasures' is a big part of the problem. We all know that what we can't have we want more of. The things that we consider to be 'off limits' are typically the things we have the hardest time limiting. And, that distance makes the heart grow fonder...especially when we're talking about chocolate. But, when we take away the restrictions and prohibitions around 'guilty pleasures', our cravings and feelings of deprivation wane. Now, plenty of people will argue that allowing yourself to let loose 10% of the time is self-sabotage, and if we're dealing with a true addiction, allergy or intolerance, then I concur. But, in most cases when we impose a zero tolerance for something, we actually create an obsession with the thing we're attempting to avoid. And, that my friend, is surely self-sabotage.

Even when I was much younger, a big partier and a raging alcoholic, I intuitively struck this balance between overdoing and then undoing, or as I would say, "I detox so, I can retox." Stupid, I know. I distinctly recall a trip to Vegas in college with a co-ed group of twenty of my closest friends. I drank and ate and smoked and did everything I wanted…to excess.

But, every morning that anything goes party girl got up and helped her body recover. I made myself (and my partners in crime) concoctions of psyllium, activated charcoal, bentonite clay, milk thistle seed extract, dandelion root extract, fennel, ginger, and turmeric. I would drag everyone to the hotel's Far-Infrared sauna to detoxify, armed with jugs of water and dry brushes. I knew that I was poisoning my body and that I was either going to put myself in an early grave or look like the walking dead long before I did, but I was also having too much fun to stop. So, I became a sponge for all things antioxidant, anti-aging, anti-inflammatory, etc., in order to try to mitigate the price my body and mind were paying for my rock 'n roll lifestyle. The more I learned, the more I wanted to rebuild and repair my body and mind and the less I wanted to tear them down.

Now, you may be thinking that I've forgotten an entire category of toxins, the kind we often find in high concentration in our relationships. I assure you, I have not. And it is not that I just haven't gotten to them yet or because they're any less toxic. In fact, for many of us, they are *the* most toxic thing in our lives. They can also be the most involved toxins to process and shift. So, because one of the quickest ways to set up a goal for failure is to start by focusing on the hardest or biggest part of it, I recommend starting small and working our way up to the bigger life detoxes. These may include jobs, relationships with others, relationships with money, past trauma toxicity, and so on. Except for in extenuating circumstances, those are not the things that I recommend people detox first.

While it may seem like an oversimplification, the best indicator of *if* you will achieve any goal is if you have started actively working towards it. It's Newton's first law of motion, "an object at rest will stay at rest, and an object in motion will stay in motion." So, our first goal in detoxing, and one of the most important roles I play with my clients, is to get the ball rolling.

Once that first little ball of snow is formed and starts rolling downhill, it will keep going unless something stops it in its tracks. In the beginning, it doesn't take much for it to get stuck, but as it rolls, it picks up more and more snow, more and more speed, and gets bigger and heavier, and harder to stop.

The same is true with deconstructing our toxic burden. We start with something small that we feel really confident we can knock out fast and get one under our belt right out of the gate.

I call this first detox goal the virgin goal, and there are three simple criteria for what a virgin goal must be:

1- it must be something you KNOW you can accomplish quickly

2- it must be something that you're excited to do, not dreading

3- it must be something meaningful...even though it has to be a sure thing, it also has to be something that you'll be proud to have accomplished in order for it to create momentum

To get to your virgin goal, first, make your list. This should be a stream of consciousness brain dump of all the things you want to be able to check off your detox goals list. This is something that I work with my clients to help brainstorm and would be happy to help you create too. This list will include everything from the super simple and obvious, like achieving your ideal daily water intake, to the big, hairy, audacious goals, like escaping a toxic work environment. To help you get your list rolling, a link to some of the most common detox goals that show up on my clients' lists can be found in my Instagram Bio @theantiagingjunkie

Here are some key guidelines for making your list:

Do not try to put your detox goal items in order of big to small as you are making it.

Do not judge, question, filter, or edit your goals. If they pop into your head, capture them and move on. Just get them all down on paper (or on a computer).

This list-making activity is in itself a significant part of processing, integrating, and detoxing. A gross but effective way to think about this is 'puking it on paper'; the process itself should feel cathartic

If it feels stressful instead, stop, take some deep breaths and remind yourself of these truths:

- Putting these goals on paper does not obligate you to do any of them, and whether you complete all of them or none of them is not the point of the exercise, nor is it of any consequence whatsoever at this moment
- This list is for you and for your eyes only; let yourself surrender and release any and all thoughts, ideas, and beliefs about the things that you feel are toxic in your life onto this list
- Remember that once completed, what you do with this list is entirely up to you. You can move onto the next step (which I will share in just a minute), you can seal it in an envelope and stick it in a drawer, or you can rip it to pieces, set it on fire, or flush it down the toilet. Knowing that you can destroy this list once you've made it will help you feel more freedom to write anything and everything, without shame, fear, judgement, or reservation.
- Remember that no matter how personal, intimate, scary, embarrassing, or overwhelming the contents of your list may be, they are universal. If they are on your list, you can be certain that they are being experienced by others too.

- Remember that the act of writing this list alone is like releasing a pressure valve, and in doing so, you are, in fact, accomplishing your virgin detox goal. Surprise!

Once you have your list (if you have chosen to proceed and it has not been incinerated or flushed), you will then cull your list in a specific way that makes it super simple. Note: You are NOT going to have to organize your entire list!

- Pick a highlighter, preferably in a color that makes you happy
- Read through your list quickly and for each item, ask yourself, 1- 'would this be relatively quick and easy to start doing?' and 2- 'do I feel any dread around doing this?'
- Highlight the things that you feel could be relatively quick and easy to do and that you don't dread doing. *don't overthink this, trust your gut, and don't spend more than 10 seconds on each item
- Then, put those items into their own list, which I call 'The Freeway' on a separate page, and park everything else in a different list, which I call 'The Parking Lot'
- If your Freeway list has more than five items on it, then cull it down further by picking the top 5 things that you are MOST excited to do/get done. Move all but those five to the top of your Parking Lot list
- Then for your final five detox goals, imagine what it will be like to do each and what it will feel like when each one is done (close your eyes to help the visualization process and spend no more than thirty seconds max on each goal)
- After having felt into all five goals, pick the ONE that you feel most interested in doing now!
- This is what I've coined, your siphon goal. The idea of a siphon goal is powerful because it's so visual. So, if you can't visualize a siphon, stop reading now and go watch a short siphoning video on YouTube. It takes a little bit of effort to get a siphon going, but once you get it flowing, it's

all downhill from there, AND the amount of liquid that you can siphon is pretty much infinite. It's a powerful force, and the same applies to your detox goals. Your siphon goal is the gateway goal. It opens up the floodgates, and guess what? Once it's complete, you go straight back to your Freeway list, pick your next detox goal and start it immediately. The Freeway list literally frees the way for your momentum to continue and for that snowball of compounding detox accomplishments to get bigger, faster, more confident, and more capable.

- When you have checked off four of the five detox goals on your Freeway list, it is time to go back to your Parking Lot list.
- Scan through your Parking Lot list quickly and for each goal again, ask yourself, 1- 'would this be relatively quick and easy to start doing?' and 2- 'do I feel any dread around doing this?'.
- From the highlighted items, cull those down to the five you are most excited about...and, Voila, you have your new Freeway list ready to jump straight into once you've completed the final goal from your last list.
- A couple of notes here:
- As you are moving through your Freeway lists and gaining momentum, new goals will arise. It's inevitable as you begin to feel better, gain confidence and learn more. Do not lose these new goals! You can either pop them in your Parking Lot list if you don't feel that they are urgent, or you can fast-track them straight into your Freeway list to tackle next. This is all part of the snowball effect that will have you accomplishing your goals like never before.

I am a firm believer that if we choose, we can become 1% better every day. Imagine then what you could achieve in 100 days...100% improvement. Imagine what you could achieve in a year. The reason that the Parking Lot to Freeway approach I have created is so successful is that it shifts the focus from achieving the big goal to tackling tiny incremental and compounding goals that you celebrate every single step of the way.

Just as the tiny incremental increases in temperature are imperceptible to the frog and are therefore not painful, this process of incremental detoxification can make the pain of the big detox practically imperceptible as you move toward it gradually. While that is a big piece of why this works, it can also make it difficult to be fully aware of your progress. That is why it is crucial to long-term success and sustainability that you keep some sort of log or measurement of how you're feeling, doing, looking, moving, etc. When we have an awareness of our improvements and acknowledge our progress, we maintain our motivation and momentum and continue to get more of the same.

Document how you feel at the starting point of each detox goal and document how you are feeling as often as you can along the way. Do whatever works best for you; take pictures, keep a journal, share with an accountability partner or coach if you'd like, but observe, observe, observe! It is helpful to rank specific measures that are important to you every day so that you can track your progress as well as pivot your approach if progress slows. For example, like the boiling frog, many of us have forgotten what it feels like for our bodies and minds to be at ease vs. dis-ease. We may have had headaches for years, and because they have been chronic, we can't even recall what it felt like without them. As we gradually move through our detox goals, long-standing ailments and other complaints will gradually dissipate and in many cases completely disappear. Monitoring how we are feeling allows us to be fully aware when that decades-old back pain or arthritis suddenly is no longer present. You will essentially be unboiling your frog, bringing it back from the brink of danger very slowly, and that's exactly how you want it.

If you've been certified in SCUBA, you know that when you ascend to the surface, you have to do so very slowly and methodically so that you do not surface too quickly. If you do come up too fast, you will suffer from decompression sickness, aka: 'the bends'. While it's nice to get to the surface quickly when you want to, going up too fast will make you sick. And, as tempting as it is to detox quickly, that too can make you sick.

So, document how you feel now (your baseline) and then track how you are feeling as you go through the items on your Freeway list. Each time you look back, you'll be amazed at just how far you have come.

It may be a big, toxic world out there, but the incredible and true news is that you are in control of the toxicity you allow into YOUR life. With a little time and diligence, you can take back control of your external and internal worlds and be your own sovereign remedy. If you would like help navigating the path back to ultimate wellness, myself and the other incredible co-authors of this book are here for you. Happy healing!

ABOUT THE AUTHOR
AMANDA SULLIVAN

Amanda Sullivan, aka: The Anti/Aging Junkie, is the founder of Vital Beauty, a consultancy for holistic wellness and degenerative dis-ease prevention. Over the past 25 years Amanda has overcome a myriad of personal health crises, including Systemic Candidiasis, depression, alcohol, substance and anxiety addiction, hormonal hair loss/alopecia and stress-induced Adrenal fatigue. Today, she taps into her wealth of personal experience, research and recovery to help others detox their lives and live richer and fuller with vibrance, joy and vitality.

Amanda lives in Maryland with her husband and daughter where they are currently working on plans for their dream home; a non-toxic haven that is one with the gorgeous, natural environment surrounding them. A habitat that is more glass, light and air than walls. Where health, love and joy radiate like the sun streaming through the lush canopy of leaves above them.

Follow Me:
Instagram: @theantiagingjunkie
Clubhouse: @antiagingjunkie
Websites: theantiagingjunkie.com
 thevitalbeautysource.mymonat.com
Contact me:
theantiagingjunkie@gmail.com

BRITTANY YOUNG

LANDING SOULFULLY

Have you ever felt like you truly needed to surrender every part of yourself because you truly had nothing left to give?

Have you ever taken a second to see that your pain is your medicine?

Do you ever think about how wonderful life would be if you accepted all parts of who you are inside and out?

If you answered "**YES**" to any or all of these questions, then this chapter is for you!

WHY WE EXIST

*M*y mission during this lifetime is to move women from the mind of doing to being within one's own soul. The soul is the infinite self which is completely connected to universal energy. But, Houston, we have a problem! Post-traumatic pain points are at the forefront of our challenges right now. We are constantly at war within our own bodies, and all around us, the world is changing rapidly.

We find ourselves:

- Listening to others and looking for external validation rather than internal
- Giving our power away, which blocks our awareness and emotions, the entryway to the soul
- Trying to control every situation and how we feel
- Creating action and stories from the mind which cause us to feel lost, unseen, and unsupported

When we feel lost, we lose sight of our infinite self, and we don't live from the soul. We would rather fight against criticism to prove our worth and belonging than follow our feelings and emotions. We operate from fear rather than our purposeful passion. In fact, the deeper layer here is we allow slavery consciousness and scarcity to take over the mind thus creating separation in our very being.

We search for someone else to fix our problems, but this only proves to be short lived.

If we do not believe we are perfect in the Divine, we lose sight of our greatness. We fall victim to fear, resentment, judgment, anxiety, and we go against our own true nature. We think everything needs to be perfect. Perfection leads to procrastination, doubt, and comparison. We then don't feel good enough to measure up to societal standards, and then we wind up judging other people. Who we are really judging is ourselves. We eliminate self-love, self-care, and self-worth.

How about looking deep within what the soul wants and what it is capable of?

When we are in our essence, also known as radical self-acceptance, we don't need to look outside of ourselves to know we have the power to BE. We allow ourselves to choose based on awareness. When we are aware, we synchronistically attract others into our lives who uphold the same beliefs or new ways of teaching that we want to learn from.

What I want to call your attention to is that if you place trust and faith that God/Source/Love energy's plan is always right, you will never have a worried day in your life! My friend, we are not running the show because it's Love's will not ours. The best part is you are offered a spot to bathe in a beautiful ocean of love with the Divine. Life becomes simple when we trust our Creator of Love to lead us because, Darling, it's Life on Life's Terms. Let go of the mind fuckery, and allow the Divine Intelligence to bring true bliss and freedom into your life! What this requires is a spiritual transformational experience! What would that do for you, my love?

I must tell you, not every experience I had was one of blessed remembrance. I've been stripped and entered into what we call the dark night of the soul. I refer to it often as a recalibration or restructuring built by Love. I'd love to share this story with you because maybe you personally hit a wall now or in the past. You were unsure and uncertain of why this happened to you of all people. Let me tell you, my sweet friend, that's exactly what I thought, "*Why me?*" How could life do this to me?

THE BOTTOM OF ALL BOTTOMS

I was on my hands and knees, looking up to the ceiling. "Do you not see my eyes?" I was pleading with Love asking for forgiveness, asking for Him, and wondering when this pain was going to stop. I remember crying out, "I cannot do this anymore! I cannot continue with these choices in my life. If I do, I'm going to die. Please help me!" I did not want to die on my bathroom floor after ten years of drinking. I could barely look at myself in the mirror. My eyes were sunken in, my face felt burnt and dry like leather, my nails were completely brittle, and I gained about 50 pounds over those many hard fought years. I truly thought I was alone and God was absent like everyone else who abandoned me because I was an alcoholic.

At 17, I took one drink and knew instantaneously I had a problem with alcohol. I was warned it was a disease I was born with, and the only way to get rid of it was to never pick it up, stop if I did pick it up, or die trying. My drinking career began after a sexual assault in the back seat of a car. After the incident occurred, I never told a soul. I lived with the pain for 13 years before I released the information, along with the other abuse I suffered from when I drank.

Somehow I managed to become a high-functioning alcoholic throughout college and my professional career, but I didn't hide it very well. Showing up hungover or still drunk at work, I was fired from my first corporate job in the pharmaceutical industry, blew through $30,000 in 2 years, and almost lost my first home I purchased at 23. I could not manage my drinking, my food addiction was at the top of its game, and I was suicidal.

After several relapses, a few near-death experiences, and losing all of my friends and family one by one because of my disease, I realized I had a choice: get clean or die. I called my father and asked for help. All he could offer me was, "Just stop drinking," and I thought to myself, 'How am I going to do this on my own?' It turns out I wasn't alone through any of this.

Although drinking was my escape from reality, Love never left my side. She stayed with me during this phase of "nothingness." Why? Nothingness is the greatest part of the movie right before the hero or heroine is triumphant. She surrenders all that she possesses. She lets go trying to do everything her own way and by herself.

Love may seem absent, and we're left to die trying, but that's the thing; it's not about trying in this space. Not knowing what is next is the most intimate part of the human experience. You're able to release all of your expectations you placed upon yourself and give them to Spirit. Remember too, you cannot rush Love! You truly aren't meant to know everything, and even when you think you do, God changes the plan! This part of life is a true test of trust. Do you trust this Higher Power with your life? When you have nothing left to give and feel like giving up on yourself, do you trust Her? It is here in the void that is your greatest asset.

Even when God is absent, God is present. You're given a choice of how you want to see life unfold. I'll tell you the blessings you receive when you give up and trust far outweighs anything you could possibly imagine. Life is being reordered and rebuilt. Keep the trust and faith because there is so much beauty and peace waiting for you on the other side.

MY LIFE'S WORK TODAY

Today, by the grace of Spirit, I am 8 years sober. I no longer answer to anyone in the corporate world. I started my own business in 2017, and I haven't looked back since. I first began personal training after being let go from a sales position within oil and gas. Within the first month of beginning my own business, I had a full book of business with 20 clients. But I knew this wasn't the end result for me. God was leading me to my true purpose, and coaching people in recovery from addiction was part of that path. Listening to my intuition and Spirit, my career went through several iterations as an entrepreneur. Four years into coaching, I can finally say that I am home in my business.

I am a Soul Activation Channel for women of Power, Wealth, and Influence. I help these beautiful women move away from self-sacrifice and expectation to commit to a life of pleasure in the areas of their businesses, marriages, and the relationship with themselves. As a Channel to the Divine Intelligence, I open my soul up to receive guidance from Love. I do not plan most of my work because it is Spirit and soul-led. This gives the client an opportunity to experience connection with their deepest feelings, notice the subtle differences of control rather than surrender, and we work on the gift of receiving from the feminine ocean of Love.

I'd love to share "Veronica's" story with you all. Veronica came to me in December of 2020 wanting to change the way she was showing up in her business. Veronica worked with a business coach to try to crack the code on how she needed to be more of a presence online, show up for her audience 24/7 and make a million dollars. So why did she want to hire *me?* She already made over $300,000 in 2020. She was also a best-selling author, international speaker, and rocking it in her financial business, yet she sought me out? To say the least, I was honored to be the one to lead her through this energetic process.

As we started working together, I found out this gorgeous soul truly lacked confidence and placed a million expectations on herself even the Dali Lama wouldn't be able to meet! Have you ever done that? You placed so many "to-dos" in your notebook, and by the end of the day, half of them weren't yours to even do?

We came to the conclusion that the list needed to be chucked in the trash the moment we started our work together. How was she going to be on her way to $1 million in revenue in 2021 if she was weighed down by her list? Veronica began to grant herself the permission that her heart was her first priority. She said to me, "I am ready to be led, and I am willing to be led. Please show me what the next steps are in order to move forward!"

And so began the year long process of radical self-acceptance with Veronica's soul. (*Note, I am writing this in April 2021, and we were four months into working together*). January was a month of shedding all of the bullshit layers keeping Veronica safe. We needed to understand her core wound of unworthiness which was caused by a lack of confidence in childhood. We did energy healing and emotional clearing because her energy was tied into her father's lack of worthiness of himself. We also picked up that she was carrying burdens from her mother that simply made her feel a lack of safety.

After clearing out these energies, she made adjustments in her business by hiring a new employee. This allowed Veronica to bring in $20,000 for herself. In February, we experimented with seeing how it felt to push the envelope in her business. She booked 15 media appearances during that month, several speaking engagements, and not to mention she was birthing a new project for women to recognize their ability to be wealthy in all areas of their life. During the month of February, Veronica was tested by her father. He made her an offer to be part of his firm again, and he said he would double her salary. Veronica refused to give her power away at that moment. She wasn't driven by the money, and from that day forward, her energy shifted even when she showed up to speak with me. Her revenue grew to $39,000 that month, and she did something only we can dream of doing. SHE TOOK MONDAY'S AND FRIDAY'S OFF! Yes, you read that right! How can someone make more money and work less? Continue reading, and you'll find out!

In March, I asked Veronica to experiment again, but this time she was not allowed to plan anything. This was extremely uncomfortable for her. We were still working on deconstructing childhood beliefs, rules, and expectations, and I was asking a FINANCIAL PLANNER NOT TO PLAN! March also happened to be when things in her personal life went sideways. Her husband started questioning this "new woman" and why she was working more on her spirituality than her business. Breaking the rules within her industry allowed Veronica to let her hair down and be herself. Why couldn't others, especially the man she married, see that was her truth?

The one person who didn't believe it to be true was Veronica herself! How could this be if she were excited to share all of her gifts with everyone? Veronica needed to introspectively look deeper within and dig into trust. The first two months we spent rebuilding an unshakeable confidence and destroyed the belief of unworthiness. What was needed was a giant pause. Yes, you read that right, a pause! I asked Veronica to stop leaving her soul behind, and on the days when she wasn't working, was it possible to sit with her human self and ask the soul what she wanted. After much-needed rest in the ocean of feminine love, Veronica took a big breath, looked me in the eyes, and made a decision to sit with her heart. On April 1st, 2021, she messaged me to let me know she made $54,000 working three days a week, raising two children, and running a household. You could imagine the grin on my face after that message! Veronica continues today to use the power of the pause, and together we named it The Permission Process of Radical Self-Acceptance.

DARLING, YOU'RE WORTHY OF RECEIVING

The Permission Process of Radical Self-Acceptance helps women embody and accept all of their past choices so they can truly love themselves entirely. There are four areas to cover within this process. They are Descension, Reordering, Power of Pause, and Receiving Trust. We will now cover each part of the process a bit more in-depth.

1. **Descension**, also known as the Dark Night of the Soul, is the space where everything is stripped from you. You're left with literally nothing. You may take this personally, and it seems as if you're the only one experiencing this pain. This is the place on the bathroom floor when you're crying out, asking why this is happening to you! Most of us fight this position we are in and tend to think we can push our way out of it. No, hunny, this is actually a place where Love is taking you for a reason. If we fight this stage, we will be here for months, maybe even years. It is here I meet my clients because something is starting to unravel, and there is no room for control. Press pause on your doing here because you're about to open the channel of feelings!

2. We begin opening up the channel of these feelings and create an individual plan to break down the feelings. This is the phase of **Reorder**. This is where our energy starts to break down, and sometimes we experience a full spiritual death. At this point, everything feels as if it is unraveling, but in reality, *Love is trying to burst through every little crack*. We need to crumble here in order to be made whole again. We are made ready here for the next stage, which is **Pause.**

3. **The Power of Pause** for me personally is the greatest stage to be in because it allows you to ask yourself, "How much do I trust

Spirit with my life? How much am I willing to do *nothing* and give up full control in order to prepare myself for *receiving* more than I asked for?" When we take time to pause, we are truly humbled. How much more can be taken away from you? Are you ready to trust the Divine that everything will unfold perfectly when you're not running the show? We take time to connect with our hearts each day because pausing teaches us the beauty lies within us; unconditional love and support are your superpowers. The pause is the space of freedom to welcome your human into a spiritual experience and feel the depths of God's love for you. This stage looks different for each one of us, and it may last longer for you than it will for someone else. Do not compare your process to another here. Allow the Divine to soothe you in this phase of nothingness. This is where you are rebirthed. You're on the precipice of receiving for the rest of your life. The last stage of the Permission Process is to trust what you receive.

4. Last but certainly not least, we lean into **Receiving Trust**. It feels as if we went from death to redemption. Our energetic capacity opens us up to awareness. We start to truly celebrate ourselves like never before. We are not worried about expectations, deadlines, or money coming in. We are in complete TRUST here with our Creator. It is through Trusting Love we allow God to take over our lives, we step away from control, and it is here we find strength. You are allowed to float here and let God do what She wants with you. You're the middle manager from now on, and Source is the CEO. Your pain becomes your medicine and your message. You give yourself permission to feel your heart and let her speak to you until she is seen, heard, and supported.

You are worthy of giving yourself permission to let go of control and expectations. If you're tired of sacrificing your time, energy, and relationships, allow the Divine to sweep you off your feet. You were not taught this in school or by your guardians. When we were children, we often felt in order for us to receive love we needed to be right. We now know after reviewing the Permission Process that letting go and letting Love give to us is the most powerful gift of all. And remember, this process of Descension, Reordering, Power of

Pause, and Receiving Trust can be implemented and applied to all areas of your life.

WHY PERMISSION WORKS

In January of 2021, I started playing with how I wanted to show up in my business. New and existing clients were coming to me, and I did not have to chase anyone. I felt as if it were going to be my year of financial freedom until, out of the blue, a client decided to quit two months into a yearlong contract of working together. I tried to salvage the relationship, but I honestly went into full panic. 'What would other coaches in my industry think of me? Does this make me a terrible human and awful mentor? Am I not good enough at my work? Why is she quitting on me? Why can't I be the one to end this relationship?' I spiraled into a thousand thoughts that did not sit kindly with this other soul. It was a negative energetic exchange forcing me to experience spiritual death in my business, marriage, relationships with others, and myself. It took me about six weeks to recover from this breakup before finding myself in the first stage of descension. The biggest lesson here was giving myself permission to do the inner work. If I declined to work directly with Spirit, I do not believe I'd give myself a chance to fully feel my feelings. I am not even sure this chapter of this book would be born either! Lying in a puddle of tears allowed me to bring this process forward, and I feel honored to share it with you. Shall you wish to inquire more information, please feel free to contact me and visit my website BrittanyYoungWealth.com. We can book a Spiritual Visionary Session to connect directly with Spirit on what your soul needs clarity on before you're granted permission to move forward.

MY GIFT TO YOUR SOUL

The Permission Process of Radical Self-Acceptance is more than the four stages you experience. It is an in-depth spiritual awakening you fully embody on your human journey. To summarize:

1. Even when you feel like giving up, hand over all of your pain to Source.

2. Allow Love to reorder your life.

3. Through nothingness, you are given time to pause and re-emerge when Spirit says you are ready.

4. Trusting Love's plan with your life, let go of the control and hand over the keys to the bus; you're not responsible for driving anymore.

When we start to trust God, all the pain, control, expectations, overwhelm, you name it, push us to the brink of surrender. We start to radically accept all parts of ourselves almost in a dramatic fashion. We start to blow bubbles, do cartwheels in the street again, and wear side ponytails in our hair. This is the space you are meant to be in, my love—the place of intimacy with your heart. If you learned nothing from this chapter, know this: I see you. I hear you. I love you. I truly do from the deep depths of my soul. You're so worthy and deserving of Love.

Are you ready, open, and willing to receive?

LEADING YOU IN LOVE

You are not alone
You are so supported
Breathe life into yourself
Breathe the life that is around you
Stay in complete and utter curiosity

Only you know the answers when you trust that you're being provided for

I am here
I am safe
I am protected
I am loved

Thank you
Thank you
Thank you
I love you
I love you
I love you
And so it is🖤

ABOUT THE AUTHOR
BRITTANY YOUNG

Brittany is a Soul Activation Channel helping Women of Power, Wealth, and Influence out of sacrificial hustle and head and into their playful hearts & pleasure. Brittany is helping her clients trust their hearts again and receive love from the Divine. She gives her clients permission to radically love and accept themselves through The Permission Process.

Brittany spent 15 years in the pharmaceutical industry working with CEOs, top executives and closed multi-million dollar deals in sales. In 2017, Brittany started her own business and let her Guides and her gut literally lead her into the work she is producing today on this planet.

Today, Brittany works with women in the financial sector, doctors, lawyers and women in corporate.

Email: Information@brittanyparsonscoaching.com
Website: www.BrittanyYoungWealth.com
Book a Spiritual Visionary Session https://calendly.com/
brittanyyoungwealth/spiritual-visionary-session
www.brittanyyoungwealth.com

KELLY KINGSLAND

THE JOURNEY

*M*y journey into the world of energy began in 2010. I discovered a documentary called 'No One Dies in Lily Dale'. It changed my life.

For those that aren't familiar with Lily Dale, it is a gated community in New York State and is renowned as the epicentre of the Spiritualist movement in North America. To live there, you must be a member of the Spiritualist church, and a number of its residents are either mediums or healers. All must go through rigorous testing to be approved to work within the gates.

At the time, I wasn't sure why it happened (now I know it was the Universe pushing me along), but when I watched the documentary, all I could think about was getting to Lily Dale. It wasn't a simple curiosity. It was a deep-seated need to go. I was being compelled, and I didn't know why.

I booked a trip, and as soon as I passed through the gate of the community, my soul felt like it had come home. It has been an ongoing love affair ever since.

In May of 2011, I decided to attend a 3-day workshop being offered through a Spiritualist church located just outside the Lily Dale grounds. This weekend would change the trajectory of my life. I just didn't know it at the time.

This intensive weekend retreat consisted of learning about mediumship, meditation, and energy healing. While I had enjoyed receiving mediumship readings in the past, meditation and energy healing were a whole new world to me. I loved every second of it.

During our hands-on practice of energy healing, I was performing healing on a gentleman, and he asked me if I was a Reiki practitioner. I told him I wasn't. I didn't even know what it was! He shared with me that he was trained in Reiki and explained that the energy of those that do Reiki feels different than those that do other healing methods and that my energy gave off a Reiki vibration. His exact words to me at the time, and I will never forget them, were, "If you don't do Reiki, you should." I tucked that bit of information away and thought nothing more of it.

On the same weekend, the teacher and head of the church pulled me aside and suggested I find a mediumship development class when I get home to develop and strengthen my connection to Spirit. I agreed that I would look into it.

Fast forward a few weeks later. I was on my computer at work, and I remembered what was said. I did a bit of research on what Reiki was and how it worked. I was intrigued, so I searched for Reiki teachers near me. One of the first results was a woman with a big smile and a very kind face. I felt a connection, so I read on.

As I reviewed her class offerings, I saw she offered weekly Development classes, as well as all levels of Reiki through to Master/Teacher. I continued scrolling down the page and was stunned to discover she lived eight houses away from me. I can see her house from my door. I thought there had to be a mistake, so I called her and said, "Do you live on ___ street? At the corner of ____ and ____?" She replied, "Yes." I started laughing and told her we were neighbours. We had lived near each other for 20 years and never met!

If there was ever evidence of the Universe directing you EXACTLY where you are meant to go, this was it! I immediately signed up for her classes, and she is my Reiki Master and mentor.

When I was doing my Reiki Master/Teacher class, I met a fellow healer named Tammy (not her real name). We had an instant connection, and I honestly think we had a past life relationship. Little did I know her purpose was to teach me a hard lesson. We decided we were going to change our little part of the world and opened up a space together that focused on energy healing services. We both provided Reiki, and we hired a massage therapist and a reflexologist. We had guest mediums come in to do readings, taught classes, and had a retail component with crystals, incense, and the like. We had the best time! The energy was positive, and our friendship grew.

About four months into the venture, I noticed that we had differing ideas on responsible financial business practices. We were both strong personalities, but only one of us knew how to compromise. We started arguing, and the business started suffering. Tammy told me it was my fault and that my money-focused energy was causing all of the issues.

At that point in time, I decided to cut my losses and leave the business. All I asked was to be bought out of my half of the furniture and equipment. Needless to say, that didn't go over well. Of course, Tammy didn't have the money to do that, so I offered to take half of the furniture instead. If looks could have killed me when I moved my share out of the building, I'd be dead ten times over. The knot I felt in my stomach was almost enough to make me sick. In all honesty, I brought a friend with me to 'help' me move the furniture, but really, it was because I knew if I were there alone, there would be one hell of a confrontation, and I couldn't deal with that. At the time, I didn't realize what a profound effect this experience was having on me.

Because of the negativity and trauma of the partnership breaking down, I decided to step away from energy work for a bit. I couldn't service my clients properly if doing Reiki brought up negative feelings. Thus ended my journey. Or so I thought. I returned my focus to being a mom and wife and returned to a full-time job. And the years passed...

Fast forward four years. I hadn't done Reiki in 4 years. Wow. What a waste!

In the fall of that year, my youngest child moved away to University. My baby. The dread was immense, and I began to mourn his leaving months before he left. Empty Nest Syndrome was sinking its claws into me, and I was so disconnected from myself and my energy, I didn't even notice.

The move-out day arrived, and I kept a strong face on, all the while I was frozen with fear on the inside. I moved him into his residence apartment, and when we were done getting him set up, he walked me down to the car to say goodbye. I was strong until I got in the car. Then the floodgates opened. I cried the whole 1½ hour drive home (which, in hindsight, probably wasn't the safest situation). I didn't stop crying for a month. At that point, I decided to get some help. I met with a therapist, and I cried some more.

One evening I was sitting in my living room trying to decide what I wanted to do now that both of the kids were gone. I had every evening to myself, and drowning in sorrow wasn't productive. I was overeating and drinking a little too often. That's when I met my coach, and she saved me.

I was a lightworker, and I wasn't using my gifts the way I was meant to. It was time to get back into Reiki, but I couldn't. There was no energy happening anywhere. I was a dead circuit. After a brief moment of panic, I called my Reiki teacher and told her what was happening. She suggested I go in for a 'touch-up' attunement. So, I did. And... nothing. I thought back to my 'divorce' from my business partner and realized my body blocked my energy when that whole ordeal happened.

I talked to my coach about it, and I decided to just ease back, continue with the program I was doing, and see what happens. We cleared the root chakra, and nothing. We cleared the sacral chakra, and nothing. Then we hit the solar plexus. That was a bad one. It took a lot of work and a lot of tears, but I managed to unblock it. The release was almost orgasmic. I could physically feel the blockage leave. I felt lighter, freer, and more myself than I had in a very long time. The energy came flowing back like a river. I was vibrating. It was so intense! Immediately, and without her permission, which I would normally never do, I did a distance reading on my coach. I told her about it the next day, and it was spot on. Thank goodness!

I put a very vulnerable post out over Facebook and told some of my story. I asked for volunteers because I was out of practice. They lined up for their free energy/chakra readings. I was back and stronger than ever.

At that point, I realized how damaging blocked chakras and energy could be to an individual physically, mentally, and emotionally. A lot of people don't even know they're blocked or what the chakras do. People need information and education. They can't fix it if they don't know what's broken.

I've been told my 'superpower' is that I possess both a scientific and intuitive understanding of the human mind, which I'm able to use to help my client's live life to their fullest potential WITHOUT being hindered by inauthentic belief systems and the expectations and demands placed upon them by others.

I've developed programs that focus on using the person's energetic body to release blockages, limiting beliefs, and past trauma. While helping women from all over the world, I discovered the relationship between a body's energy and the impact it can have on a person's business. It's amazing how we can block ourselves from reaching the next level in our business and our lives without being aware we are doing it. I began working with women from both a personal and career perspective, with clients from homemakers to high-level CEOs. I've also trained dozens of people in the art of Reiki. Bringing new healers into our world is my passion.

One of the first things I do with a client or student is to teach them about their personal energy and how it works. Quite often, when they begin to learn about the effects of energetic blockages, they can identify and relate what they've been feeling and experiencing to the effect of stagnant energy. When that energy is cleared and flowing beautifully, we can begin moving into the programs that help them uplevel. Whether that be discovering what their soul's purpose is on this plane, incorporating magick and rituals to expand their consciousness and harness the power of manifestation, or translating the blockages as they relate to their business and/or career, watching them integrate and expand truly brings me joy.

ENERGY 101

The energetic body is made up of numerous chakras, but there is a main meridian that runs from the top of your head to the base of your spine and within that are seven main chakras.

The first chakra, which is located at the base of your spine, is the root chakra. The root chakra is all about security and safety. It's very much linked to the psychosocial age of infancy. Are you loved? Are you safe? Do you have a roof over your head, with all the very necessities for survival? We often find that people with blocked root chakras grew up in a household that didn't feel safe. They may have moved frequently, which did not permit a feeling of security. Or there were issues in the adult relationships that affected the children.

The second chakra, the sacral, which I will be referencing later when we discuss Sex Magick, is a chakra located between the pubic bone and the belly button and is the source of your sexuality, your sensuality, and your self-esteem. Abundance and manifestation are also anchored there. Abuse and insecurity can cause this chakra to be affected.

The third chakra, which is the solar plexus, is located between the belly button and diaphragm. The solar plexus is all about your personal power and your identity. The way you want to present yourself to the world is anchored in the solar plexus. Quite often, how people want the world to see them is not necessarily indicative of their true selves. It takes a tremendous amount of courage to stand up and say, "This is me!". Many of us are not confident enough to do that.

The fourth chakra is your heart chakra. It is located right where your heart is. The heart chakra is all about love for self and love for others. If the heart is blocked, it's often because there's been a dramatic loss. Perhaps there's been a loss of a parent, loss of a child, loss of a spouse, or loss of a pet. Abusive relationships that damage your self-esteem will also affect the heart chakra (as well as the sacral).

The fifth chakra is the throat chakra. The throat chakra is all about speaking your truth. It can get blocked if, for example, you are at a business meeting and when you try to contribute, someone shushes you, or if you're telling a funny story to a group of people and then all of a sudden people start talking in the middle of it. The throat chakra can become blocked when you don't feel like you're being heard. The throat chakra will respond with, "Well, if no one is listening, what is the point in talking."

The sixth chakra is the third eye chakra. It is located in between your eyes and about one inch above, on your forehead. The third eye is your connection to the psychic realm. It is your connection to Spirit. When this chakra is open, you are on point with your intuition. You are in tune with it, and you know how to listen to it. An open third eye will guide you through your daily decisions.

The seventh chakra is the crown chakra. The crown is located at the top of your head. This is your connection with the universe. This is your connection with whatever or whomever you choose to worship. This is your connection with the great unknown. When the crown is open, there is a certain unconditional trust that happens. You just know everything is going to be okay. You know you are going to get what you need. You know the universe is going to have your back.

It's not only important that we keep the chakras balanced; they must be balanced with each other. Having some chakras more active than others can cause many emotional and physical issues. I always likened the energy meridian to a sink drain. If there is a blockage, the energy can enter but can't make it all the way through. The blockage stops the flow of energy.

SO NOW WHAT?

So how do you open the chakras? There are numerous ways to open and expand the energy flowing through the chakras.

Each chakra is associated with a specific colour. They are as follows:

Root — Red
Sacral — Orange
Solar Plexus — Yellow
Heart — Green
Throat — Blue
Third Eye — Purple
Crown — Indigo or White

While I've found the most effective way to open your chakras consists of meditation and shadow work, for those not ready to delve deep into the cause of the blockages, there are other methods that, while not as effective, can yield some results.

Reiki is useful in opening chakras, however, if the issue that caused the energy stoppage is not addressed, it really is a band-aid solution. Don't get me wrong, I love Reiki, and I use Reiki daily and teach up to the Master/Teacher level. That is also why I feel confident in saying, if you plan on using methods to deal with your chakras that don't involve working on yourself and your energy, your best alternative is to be attuned to Reiki Level 1 so that you can perform daily self-treatments in order to be able to continuously treat the blocked chakras.

I am a big believer in crystals and incorporate them into my Reiki practice. If you are so inclined, crystals in the colours of the chakras can provide some assistance with blockages. So can eating the specific colour foods and surrounding yourself with the colours of the chakra in your daily life (clothing, decor, etc.).

I will, however, reiterate that the most effective way to clear the chakra is to release the event, memory, or feeling that caused the energy to stop flowing.

THE LAW OF ATTRACTION

The science behind the law of attraction is in our brains, and it is called the Reticular Activating System (RAS). The RAS is a bundle of nerves in our brainstem that filters out unnecessary information so that we can focus on the things that are important to us. A perfect example of the RAS doing its job occurs when you purchase a new car. Suddenly you start seeing that same car everywhere. They are all around you. Before you bought it, you never noticed them. That is the RAS confirming your new reality.

With the law of attraction, you call something into being by engaging the RAS. If you make a statement or a proclamation, the RAS is going to start finding proof of that for you. This is why when you're working with the law of attraction, it's important to use I AM statements. When you say things in the affirmative present, the RAS engages and will start bringing people and opportunities to your attention that you may have missed before to make your statement a reality. Your dreams and goals start coming to fruition faster because you recognize the things you need to do to make it happen.

SEX MAGICK

Part of the ability to manifest and properly practice is to ensure the chakras are completely open. The sacral, in particular, takes on a very active role in our sexuality and our expression of our sexual needs and desires.

There are two different theories when it comes to Sex Magick. The first is that by combining sexual pleasure with your dream/goal, neurologically, you're changing your brain. You are rewiring your brain so that your unconscious begins to seek out actions that are going to bring you closer to your goal (i.e. the RAS).

The second theory is that by combining the powerful sexual energy that happens during the point of climax, the energy of your dreams will be sent out into the universe. So, by expressing your dreams at the point of climax and entangling those dreams with the energy that causes it, you are blasting it out there. It's like the law of attraction on steroids.

Because like attracts like, you are going to find that an energy shift will occur that brings your dream to you. This is why the chakras must be open. If you have a blocked chakra, that energy is not going to be able to flow as needed.

I would strongly recommend energetically cleansing anything that you may use during the ritual.

If you do have a partner that you want to do this with, be very careful because you are going to be pulling their energy into what you are manifesting. If this is something that is for both of you or that you both benefit from, that is acceptable, but if their energy isn't completely aligned with yours, avoid engaging them in this practice. Be aware there is no wrong way to practice Sex Magick. You need to do what feels right for you in that time and in that moment.

The very first thing you want to do, from the ritual aspect, is to make it all about you.

What makes you feel good?
What makes you feel honoured?
What makes you feel connected to your belief system?

You can make this into a full evening with other self-care and sensory additions, or you can take 20 minutes. The choice is yours.

Start the session by visualizing the dream or goal you are trying to attract. Do not engage in physical touch at this point. Visualize it in as much detail as possible.

What are the sights?
What are the sounds?
How do you feel physically? Spiritually? Emotionally?
What vibration or energy or flavour does it bring up in your body?

You must pay close attention to that feeling. When you recognize the vibration that your dream brings to you, that's when the foreplay can start.

Enjoy the sensation, enjoy the feeling, enjoy honouring yourself and treating your body with respect, and anchoring into that feeling.

When you have completed the ritual, relax into it. Focus on what divine creation you had and feel your dream getting that much closer. Have a journal close by. You will be in that in-between state at that point, where you're open to receiving, and you want to make sure that you write it down. When you are ready, continue with your day. Disengage from the outcome. Take a step back, anchor back into your feminine energy, and release yourself from the outcome.

When you use Sex Magick as a regular practice, you become more in-tune. You become better at it, and you will find that things start manifesting more frequently.

From an introduction to energy and how to clear it to a higher-level complete energy healing vortex that will bring you into higher energetic vibrations so that you gain momentum faster, more powerfully, and stay in alignment, there are various ways we can work together to utilize energy to uplevel your business and your life.

ABOUT THE AUTHOR

KELLY KINGSLAND

Kelly Kingsland is the President/CEO of Rev. Kelly Kingsland, an Intuitive Coach, Empath, Reiki Master & Teacher, Certified Crystal Therapist and Ordained Metaphysical Minister.

Kelly works with CEOs, high-level executives and business owners, to help them blast through the energetic blocks that hold them back from scaling to the next level in their business. By combining her degree in Psychology and her intuitive/empathic abilities, Kelly possesses both a scientific and intuitive understanding of the human mind. This allows her to help her clients live life to their fullest potential WITHOUT being hindered by inauthentic belief systems and current/generational trauma.

Kelly lives near Niagara Falls, Canada, where you will find her at the beach honouring her Pisces traits.

Email: rev.kellyk@gmail.com
Website: www.kellykingsland.ca
Facebook: https://www.facebook.com/RevKellyK
Instagram:@Rev_KellyK
Clubhouse:@kellykingsland

SANDRA JOY LARATONDA

SCARCITY VS. ABUNDANCE: RAISING YOUR ENERGY CONSCIOUSNESS TO CREATE THE LIFE OF YOUR DREAMS

*H*ow many times have you woken up to your alarm blaring and wished with every ounce of your being that you did not have to go to work? Maybe you have wanted to be free of a relationship that weighed you down? You might have thought about taking a chance on something you have always wanted to do but talked yourself out of it time after time? I've been there, and I can promise you that the biggest misconception in life is that you have to accept your circumstances and live a life of mediocrity.

I'm the youngest of three girls, and I was raised in a family that had a very specific mindset on what life should look like. A large part of that was sacrificing happiness to be safe, successful, and secure. I had huge aspirations to become a performer on Broadway. I lived and breathed music, performed in local productions, and sang every chance I got. My parents discouraged that choice because it wasn't the safe and secure choice for a career that would be a guaranteed paycheck, benefits, and retirement. There were too many risks in that career, and I was told that I would not have their support if I chose to pursue that dream. I was taught that what truly made me happy was to be nothing more than a hobby at best. As a naive and penniless 18 year old, I listened to them and gave up on my dream. They decided that I should probably take the suggested "safe route" instead and study music education, become a teacher, and have a predictable and safe career.

The thing is, when your heart is not into something, it becomes tedious, even soul-crushing. I failed out of my first year at college because I was simply miserable. I continued my pattern of people-pleasing, and following my father's advice, I got a job as a secretary. I was a secretary for about a year until I absolutely could not stand it any longer and went back to college to study education and become an English Literature teacher. An acceptable career for my parents, and I liked reading. It seemed like a good enough choice. I enjoyed most of the 20 years I spent teaching high school English Literature. The content was ok, but the students were phenomenal. I noticed that I would spend as much time as I could encouraging students and bolstering their self-worth to make them see how they performed on standardized tests was not their defining factor. The world was truly at their doorstep, all they had to do was choose the path they really wanted, and it was always available to them. For them, I was the encouragement that I never got.

Then, in 2014, my world turned upside down. I had a terrible accident that caused major physical damage to my body and brain. I returned to teaching after a year and a half of surgeries, therapies, and recovery. I struggled daily. Teaching high school did not fit like it used to. Noise and interruptions crushed my brain, scattered my thoughts, and rendered me useless by 3pm. I was miserable. Yet, the thing I kept coming back to, what saved me, was my love and understanding of spirituality and energy healing. It was my passion. It was always my passion, even when I longed to perform, it was there, in the underpinnings of everything I did, and I realized that I had been doing energy work all along. It was time for me to step into my soul's purpose.

I decided that enough was enough, and I retired in 2018 at 43 years old. I was going to be a powerful example to my students by walking away from a career that I was not aligned with to follow my soul's purpose. I had no real plan in place and did not know what I was going to do with my life. What I did know was that I could breathe without a weight on my chest for the first time in my adult life. It was a powerfully scary moment, but I knew I had to surrender complete control and let my soul guide me. Then, the pieces of my life that were centered around spirituality took over, and amazing things began to happen. People began showing up who would help me on my ascension journey. The right things crossed my path, and I followed ideas and inspiration that I would have completely ignored before. I felt like a flower finally opening her petals to bloom.

Everyone has a different experience and purpose, and your story is unique to you. You are here now, reading this book for a reason. Allow your heart to speak and listen to its guiding energies to lead you to your soul's purpose. Allow yourself to climb out of the doubt and overwhelm that surrounds you and become exactly who you are meant to be. It's ok to step out of a career or relationship that is no longer aligned to you, one that is holding you back from being your best self. It's time to unlock your soul's purpose and live.

Unlocking your soul's purpose happens when you develop your energy consciousness. When you are intimately aware of the effects different energy has on your body, mind, and spirit, you will be able to shine a light on your brilliance and create miracles in your life. You will stop spinning out of control and end your perpetual state of suffering. You will be able to take back your power and stop living in a scarcity mindset.

The truth is, you are the *only* one who has the power to change your circumstances. You are the one who is in charge of designing your life, not those nagging thoughts of not being good enough. You are already good enough. There are many things that play into the development of the idea of where you are supposed to be, what you are supposed to do, and with whom you are supposed to surround yourself. Humans have a deep desire to belong, and that is why we often make choices that are not truly in alignment with our souls. This goes back to our primal brains, where we learned how to survive. Being exiled from others was a sure way to die, so we did what we had to do to ensure our survival. This survival mechanism is still within the human brain today.

This is why we have comfort zones. We feel safe in our comfort zone, and when we try to leave it, our primal fight or flight instinct kicks in and safely pushes us back to our comfort zone. This also happens with the people we choose to spend time with. When one person tries to elevate their position in life, create something better, stop dealing with negative life circumstances, the others in the group try to stop them. This can be through insults, shunning, tearing down the ego, stomping on self-worth, and introducing all things fear-based to scare the person into staying put. This is what my well-meaning parents did to me when I told them my dream of singing on Broadway. Many people allow themselves to be influenced by those closest to them for fear of losing something important (approval, security, etc.).

This scarcity thought pattern is integrated into our subconscious mind early in life. Remember the first time you played musical chairs? Picture yourself in the room surrounded by all of your friends. You are all dancing and playing and having a wonderful time when the game is about to begin. There's lively music playing, and when it stops, all you have to do is sit down on one of the many chairs arranged in a large circle. You are excitedly dancing and running around the circle with your friends, not a care in the world. The music stops, you sit down in a chair and excitedly motion for your friend to sit beside you, you catch your breath, the sounds of laughter slowly dying down, and that's when you notice it. One of your friends is still standing, a sad, defeated look on her face. She is led to the side, and at that moment, you've learned a new rule of the game. The fastest ones to the chairs survive. The slowest one is out.

The game continues, and each round loses a bit of the carefree fun. Soon, you are left with a small group of friends, and the game has become cutthroat. There is pushing and pulling, and even some yelling as the scramble for a seat occurs. You've won. Then you notice that all of your friends are sitting to the side and you are alone. The victor, the winner.

Now, think of what you had to do to sit in that winner's chair. You had to go against your natural inclination to help your friends, to save them a seat, to spread your joy. You had to push all of that down and allow negative actions to take over—or you wouldn't have won. The game is an example of an illusion that we are taught. The illusion that we must be the best, the fastest, that we must fight, struggle, and keep others down to win. This is the beginning of negative thought patterns that create feelings of being drained, trapped on a treadmill in a vicious cycle, not really going anywhere important. It doesn't have to be like that.

What's the secret to escaping this self-imposed prison? It's actually very simple. Think your way out, because your thoughts create your reality. Consider this, you had an argument with your partner, and you keep replaying it in your mind. This, in turn, negatively affects your mood. You get a flat tire on the way to work. Your boss criticizes your reports. You experience more troubling circumstances, and things continue to go wrong throughout the day. The negative, low energy that you are in attracts more of the same negative, low energy, and that means more problems and a terrible day.

Think of the opposite for a moment, you have just received a substantial raise at work and were congratulated on a job well done. You are in a fantastic mood, and your happiness is contagious. You receive compliments from strangers, your favorite parking space is open and ready for your car, and the shoe store has the latest style in stock and in your size. You complete your day by going out to celebrate and have a great time with your friends. The positive, high energetic state you are in attracts more positive, high energetic experiences, and you have a fantastic day.

The things we think have a direct impact on our outward circumstances because everything is energy. Energy attracts other energy that is just like it. Let's look more closely at the example in the previous paragraph. An argument (low vibrational energy, I'll call Scarcity) creates a negative energetic field. This negative field attracts more low vibrational experiences like the flat tire and a critical boss. However, receiving a raise (high vibrational energy, I'll call Abundance) creates a positive, energetic field. This abundance field attracts other high energy experiences like parking in your favorite spot or finding the perfect shoes. Energy attracts the same level of energy. Knowing this, being in the high energetic flow of abundance is ideal. So, how do you think positively to create a direct connection to high energetic frequencies that will attract positive experiences?

We need to tune into our emotions at a deep level. Most people are living according to beliefs that are not theirs, to begin with. Those beliefs were imprinted during an experience in which a powerful lesson was learned. Our brains chose to recognize the easy way, the path of least resistance, and avoid conflict (to our primal brain, conflict equals certain death), and we have a nice, new limiting belief that we subconsciously allow to control our choices for the rest of our lives. These are called self-limiting beliefs, and they are your biggest block to creating the life you want. These beliefs start imprinting when you are a child. You learn which actions bring praise from others and which actions bring negativity. Unless we consciously put a stop to it and replace that limiting belief with the truth of who we really are and with what we are truly capable of, we continue to repeat the same patterns. We are taught to suppress emotions because they are viewed as a weakness.

You have probably heard phrases like "control yourself" or "stop crying, or I'll give you something to cry about," these are limiting phrases that cause us to shut down our emotions and exist on autopilot. Ignoring our emotions keeps us in a state of lack. We have been trained to suppress emotions and do what we are told. That means that we ignore important emotional signals from our higher selves that are trying to create a better life full of abundance. There is only one way to stop this destructive cycle. You must learn to allow your emotions to fully happen, feel them, listen to them, and take the appropriate steps to follow them no matter how much others will judge or criticize you. Your emotions are your internal compass. It's just like walking into a room and immediately feeling like something is wrong. Emotional signals are an excellent guide.

This sounds simple enough until you experience negative situations that cause you to be triggered. A trigger is when something causes you to feel a negative emotion, and it is usually caused by previous experiences and not the actual situation at hand. For example, when you experience judgement and criticism from others, it is not a reflection of you. It is something triggering for the people who are being critical. In the past, if I saw someone being critical of another person, I would immediately step in and defend the person being criticized while showing anger toward the person doing the criticizing.

People can be triggered by an expectation of behavior or an expected reaction based on specific life experiences. I was triggered because I grew up in a home where it felt like everything I did was criticized, nothing was good enough, or ever had a pure intention. I was constantly living under a microscope of someone else's expectations and defending myself from them. This was a trigger I took with me into my adult life. I was always ready to fly into defensive combat mode, even when I was not the one being criticized. I learned that I was reacting that way because of my triggering experience, and I knew at a deep level that I never wanted anyone to have the helpless feeling that I had. That trigger put me into "fix it" mode, where I would step into situations to de-escalate the conflict whether it needed it or not.

Making others feel better about their triggers is not the way to ascend. We have become really talented at keeping people stuck in scarcity energy. Ways we do this are blaming others for our situation to release ourselves of all responsibility as the cause of the negative feelings. This is where you have the power to change things to a high energetic response.

When you react negatively in scarcity mode, you are not looking at the situation and self-reflecting on your triggered response. You are releasing all responsibility for it, and that keeps you stuck in scarcity energy. It doesn't matter who started it, what was said, or how things ended. What matters is your reaction to the triggers.

When you find yourself being triggered, the following three questions are a good way to gauge if you are stuck in scarcity energy:

1. How do you feel? Connect an emotion: Ex. Angry, abandoned, sad, worthless.

2. Why do you feel that way? Look at the action or words that caused the feeling.

3. What other times in your life have you felt that same way? This is where your past experiences come into play and can shed some major light on your trigger point.

Realizing you are triggered and connecting to your emotions is an amazing breakthrough. This allows you to see the situation for what it really is, a reflection of your triggers, and you can then release the need for a reaction at all and step into abundance mode.

Abundance energy happens when we ascend to higher spiritual versions of ourselves; however, it is not a straight line of ascent. It is a spiral that continues to loop around and revisit situations or triggers until we have mastered them. Think of a funnel. The bottom of the funnel is the narrowest part, and that is the tightest loop we can make. People living at the bottom of their spiral are constantly in scarcity energy, and they are attracting negative experiences. These people may be completely unaware that they are stuck here until they have an awakening. Once you realize that you are in control of the kind of energy you are putting out and attracting, you will begin your ascension up the spiral.

There are lessons on every level of the spiral. When a trigger is recognized and resolved, the universe just doesn't take our word for it. It will continue to bring situations to you that test that trigger.

This doesn't mean that you have slid back down the spiral. This is simply a test of your energy and reaction to the trigger on a higher level of the spiral. You may react negatively but realize the trigger and quickly turn things around, or you may not react at all (the ideal response). These tests from the universe can appear at any time, especially after you thought you had conquered a trigger. The higher you rise in your spiral, you become more energetically open to higher vibrations and positive actions. All of this is your choice, and you are in charge of shaping your reality.

When you want to shift your reality to a higher energetic level, it is necessary to take a deep look at your patterns and behaviors, so you can see where you are making the same low energetic choices and harboring self-limiting beliefs. This allows you to begin clearing them from your life and creating space to attract high energetic, abundant energy instead. This is not always a quick and easy process, and quite often, you are tossed some serious tests along the way. These tests are ways to keep you on the path of ascension and to recognize and release resistance to spiritual and energetic growth.

The pull toward your soul's purpose is strong, all encompassing, even if you do not know what it is at the moment. I invite you to connect with me to learn more about spiritual ascension, energy healing, how to navigate your energy spiral and discover your soul's purpose. Feeling and not ignoring your emotions and discovering and releasing your self-limiting beliefs are the first steps to clearing scarcity energy and inviting in abundance. I've walked this journey and know it is my soul's purpose to support others on theirs. It would be my honor to walk this journey with you.

ABOUT THE AUTHOR

SANDRA JOY LARATONDA

Sandra Joy is the founder and CEO of Healing Realms, LLC and Sandra Joy, LLC. She embraces the new energy consciousness of Earth and guides others to embrace this energy to connect and thrive in their soul purpose.

She is an Adult Indigo with a deep connection to Indigo, Crystal, and Diamond Children as well as a highly intuitive clairsentient. She is a Lightworker certified with Hands of Light, a Master Usui Reiki Practitioner, a Crystal and Color Energies Expert, a certified Hypnotherapist, certified Oracle Card reader, and a 20 year activator of Indigo and Crystal Children.

Her purpose in this lifetime is to connect with people who want to learn how to harness the power of their energy system and thrive in their soul's purpose. She lives in Pennsylvania on a small farm with her husband, son, daughter, and many animals.

Email: HealingRealms111@gmail.com
Website: SandraJoy.com
Facebook: https://www.facebook.com/groups/UnTameYourSoul
https://www.facebook.com/untameyoursoul
Instagram: @SandraJoySol
TikTok: @SandraJoySol
Clubhouse: @SandraJoySol

EVA GOULETTE

THE WORLD IS READY AND THE CHILDREN ARE WAITING

*A*t the top of a small hill overlooking a grove of birch trees, I stood with a group of five to eight- year-old children as we prepared to create sacred space. Prior to their arrival I had placed stakes to mark the four cardinal directions. As the children were new to the concept of creating sacred space, I began by explaining that I would be drumming while facing each of the four directions, then would drum as I looked up to honor Father Sky, I'd bend down and drum to honor Mother Earth, and finally, place my hand over my heart to honor the spirit within. We talked about the spirits of each direction, as well as the ancestors and helping spirits. When I felt they understood what was going to happen, I handed each of them a drum or rattle and began the process of calling in the spirits to our sacred space. The children were enthusiastic and engrossed in the activity. They closely watched every move I made, listening to every word I uttered.

Upon completion of the ceremony, I suggested we all sit down so we could discuss what had transpired. A tiny five-year-old with blue eyes and short blonde hair raised her hand. "Um...um, Eva, my brother died when he was little. When you were calling in the spirits... my brother came. He's standing over there." She pointed to the outer edges of our circle. "Can he stay and play with us today?"

And with that, my first day of Spirit Camp had begun.

Dancing Jaguar's Spirit Camp was created to help children connect to their inner world. By doing that, children start learning at an incredibly young age that, as human beings, we are made up of mind, body, and spirit. And all three of those aspects need to be nurtured and cared for so we can grow up to become healthy adults. By doing this work with children, I feel there will be a shift in child development. This is an element that we have not seen that much, there has been so much focus on children's minds and bodies, and not on nurturing the essence of who they are.

My journey started after a traumatic brain injury that completely altered the trajectory of my life. As I was recovering, I wanted to explore shamanism. I researched teachers in my state and I started studying with a woman who was a brilliant teacher. After studying with her for some time, she mentioned she had held an informal program with children in her neighborhood one summer which she called Spirit Camp. She had a lot of fun with it, but she felt it wasn't really "her thing." She was inspired to share with me because she had a sense it might be "my thing." As soon as she started telling me about it, I thought, "Whoa, that is something I would really love!"

That summer, I held one Spirit Camp with some of my friend's children. During that five-day period of time, each one of the children involved in the camp had a profound experience and said something that sounded like it would come out of the mouth of an adult, yet I was hearing a child speak the words. The wisdom I witnessed in those children completely changed the course of my life. I realized that those children still remember the connection they have to spirit, and I can help them understand that it's okay to stay open to those messages they're receiving and the connection to spirit they are experiencing. I could help them understand that they don't have to shut themselves down and conform to what society considers is normal. By embracing their gifts, their openness, and their connection to spirit, these children are going to be growing up balanced in who they are and understanding the different aspects that need to be nurtured and tended and cared for to maintain overall health.

From there, I started receiving divine guidance, always at 3:20 am, about this body of work that needs to come forward for the children of the world. At first, I thought it was a symptom of my brain injury, but over time I started trusting these messages and that I was really receiving downloads of information from Spirit, or from some source in the Universe. Over time, I was asked if I would be willing to be the voice of this work that needs to come forward for the children of the world. I agreed wholeheartedly because I had already seen the impact it was having on the very few children I had already worked with.

Once that agreement took place, I realized that this must be the reason I had survived the head-on car crash and the traumatic brain injury. This is why I am here, in my life, this time around. It is my dharma, my life's purpose, to bring forward this body of work for the children of our entire planet.

The next summer I taught a couple of Dancing Jaguar's Spirit Camps, and each summer the program grew. Parents who enrolled their children in the camp a second time said they saw growth in their children after their first camp experience. Their children possessed a wisdom about themselves and the world that they recognized as being unusual for such a young age, giving the children strong self-confidence which is so necessary in today's society.

At the end of every day at Dancing Jaguar's Spirit Camp, the children are so excited, almost as if they're on fire and can't wait to tell their parents about what they learned that day; all because they're learning about who they are and how they can contribute to this world as a spirit in a human body.

In addition to learning that we are all made up of energy, children also learn how to work with spirit helpers. We teach them how to do shamanic journeying to identify their power animal, then how to develop a relationship with that animal to access information and support from that spirit helper.

The tools that children learn at Spirit Camp are used as they face situations in their lives that children without a Spirit Toolbox in their possession would struggle with. It's a joy for me to hear from parents about how their children are utilizing the tools to help them in life.

Months after a seven-year-old girl had attended Spirit Camp, her mom contacted me for advice about how to relieve the child's anxiety at bedtime. A family member had recently passed away in her sleep, and the child was traumatized by that and terrified to go to sleep at night, fearing she might also pass away in her sleep. It had been a couple of weeks since the family member had passed away, and the bedtime routine for that family had been a chaotic struggle because the child was constantly fighting the need for sleep. The entire family was sleep deprived and miserable. The mom asked if I could suggest any tools that might help her child be able to relax at night and go to sleep.

I suggested that as their bedtime routine was winding down, the child could utilize the rattles that she made at Dancing Jaguar's Spirit Camp to call in the essence of her power animal. The child could ask her power animal to stay at the foot of her bed to watch over her during the night. She could also ask her power animal if it would be responsible for waking her up in the morning. The mom tried that the very night we communicated. The child's power animal happened to be an owl, which is a nocturnal animal. The child loved the owl and felt completely safe asking it for help. Calling in her power animal at night became part of the child's nightly routine. And, it completely changed the nighttime routine for the entire family, and they were able to return to more peaceful evenings and a good night's sleep.

An entire day at Dancing Jaguar's Spirit Camp is spent on Social Emotional Learning (SEL) curriculum, which provides the children with the opportunity to learn how to self-nurture and practice self-regulation. Some of the material from that day includes learning how to identify their inner dialogue, breathing techniques, mindfulness, guided meditations, affirmations, and more. The tools they leave with on this particular day can also support them in everyday situations that would normally fluster them. A local Montessori school has even incorporated some of the SEL curriculum from Dancing Jaguar's Spirit Camp into its classrooms and teachers are thrilled with the results they see in the children. The school received the Ursula Thrush Peace Grant to bring curriculum to the school that would promote inner peace for both the staff and children at the school.

One day, I was contacted by a young Dancing Jaguar's Spirit Camper who was getting in trouble at school for sticking his tongue out at another classmate. Each time it happened he was sent out into the hall. The boy asked me for advice concerning a breathing technique we used at Dancing Jaguar's Spirit Camp called "Peace Breath." During that breathing exercise, the children would imagine that they are holding Mother Earth in their hands. I would invite them to inhale deeply and fill their hearts with love. On their exhale, they were instructed to whisper the word "peace" and imagine themselves sending peace to Mother Earth. On their next breath, they were to think of someone they had recently had a conflict with and envision them in the palms of their hands. On their exhale, they were to whisper the word "peace" and send it to the person they had been in conflict with and they could watch that relationship slowly start to shift over time because of the energy of peace they were intentionally sending to that person. Spirit Campers understand this concept because of the work we had done in previous days about how positive and negative energy effects each of us.

The child asked if Peace Breath could be used when he's standing in the hall to help shift his relationship with the person he was sticking his tongue out at in the classroom. He wanted to know if it would work to whisper the word "peace" while thinking of his classmate. This child learned Peace Breath months earlier at Spirit Camp and was pulling it out of his spirit toolbox at a time when he knew it would be beneficial. I believe that eight-year-old child had stumbled upon the solution for world peace. Wouldn't our world be a different place if we all practiced that tool when we are in conflict with someone in our lives?

At Spirit Camp, we provide the children with an opportunity to experience what it feels like to connect energetically with Mother Nature. Every day, we connect to Mother Earth in some way. The children have been deepening their relationship to Mother Earth and are understanding it in a different way than any other nature program that they may have been involved with.

For example, Spirit Campers learn how to approach a tree and sense the energy of the tree with their palm chakras, ask the tree for permission to enter its space, and then place their hands on the trunk of the tree. They then breathe and connect their energy to the energy of the tree, meditate for a few minutes, and ask the tree for a message. There have been some amazing messages given to children over the years. One day, a child approached me after the exercise and whispered, "The tree asked me to take care of it and protect it. It thinks that the wind might blow it over." As we walked away from the tree, I looked back and let my eyes wander up to the top of it. The top third of the 50-foot tree was dead and could have snapped off in a strong windstorm. Stop here and let that sink in. The amazingness of that message the child received from a tree. We continue deepening and strengthening our connection with Mother Earth throughout Spirit Camp in many other ways, including connecting to the energy of a stone, a plant, or an animal.

When children become aware of their internal energy system and their external aura, they are able to understand on a deeper level what is meant by the expression "the web of life." Everything in the world is made up of energy, just as they are, so connecting energetically to the intelligence of a tree becomes possible. Ask a child to sit with his or her back against a tree for several minutes with eyes closed, and they will feel the energetic connection kinesthetically. As these children grow up into adults who comprehend the importance of caring for Mother Earth, we can begin to imagine a different kind of world.

The experience the children have on the last day of Dancing Jaguar's Spirit Camp is particularly powerful. They have spent five days learning how to be a spirit in a human body. One mom told me she felt her daughter went through a personal evolution in five days. Her daughter arrived at Dancing Jaguar's Spirit Camp on the first day not knowing anything about the "spirit" part of who she is. The mother was amazed that during that short period of time her daughter learned that she is made up of mind, body, and spirit, and that she's also made up of energy. She learned how to work with energy, how to work with spirit helpers, gemstones and crystals, pendulums, and dowsing rods. The daughter now had lots of tools that would help her connect to her higher wisdom. By the end of the week, she had learned how to connect to Mother Nature in a way that most children are completely unaware of. The mom stated that her child had learned things that she wanted to know, and she wished Spirit Camp had been available for her when she was a child.

After hearing many parents talk about their need to learn these tools, they started being invited to attend Dancing Jaguar's Spirit Camp with their child. By doing this, parents were enjoying a beautiful bonding experience with their child, and in addition, they would be able to share the tools and teachings with other members of their family. Because the parents were so excited about it, I expanded the teachings and Dancing Jaguar's Spirit Camp for Adults was created.

We've also created a Dancing Jaguar's Spirit Camp for Teens, so 13-17-year-olds are able to learn how to empower themselves with the same type of tools that the younger Spirit Campers learn, but in an age-appropriate way for them. Too many teenagers are struggling in today's world. By providing them with tools to connect to their inner world, we can help them manage the negative self-talk that can become such a destructive force in their lives. When teens learn there are tools they can utilize to help them shift their negative self-talk to more loving and compassionate self-talk, they develop the skill of self-compassion.

Another girl was about 11 when she came to Dancing Jaguar's Spirit Camp. She was going into a dark place and already started to cut herself as a coping mechanism. Her parents and therapist suggested that she attend Dancing Jaguar's Spirit Camp, as the therapist was familiar with the program. That child thrived all week, she was happy, engaged, and responsive to every suggestion and exercise. One day after she returned from the camp, her mom texted me, "I don't know who this child is that you're sending home to me, because she's smiling! I haven't seen my daughter smile in months. What are you doing?" I explained to the mom that I was providing the roadmap for her to do the inner work and giving her the tools to help her understand who she is. I was shining the light on the path for her to reach her inner wisdom. Her daughter was walking that path and doing her inner work.

One of the things we did at that camp, as we always do, was a guided meditation to teach the children how they can move unwanted energy through, then out of their body. At the end of the meditation, the children were asked to blow the unwanted energy into a pinecone they were holding in their hands. Later, after thanking the pinecone for providing the service of holding the energy, and the fire for transmuting it, they offered the pinecone ceremoniously to the fire at the end of the camp. The children learned that the fire would transmute the unwanted energy they had blown into the pinecone, and the energy would be transformed into a more positive form.

The ceremony had an impact on the child. The day after Spirit Camp ended, her grandmother had a stroke and was not expected to survive. She was the childcare provider for the family, and mother feared her daughter would start cutting again. She contacted me to ask for suggestions. I told her to have her daughter take out her spirit toolbox and remember what she had learned at Spirit Camp. If she needed help, she could contact me for suggestions.

The next day I received an email from the mom telling me that she was writing her email through tears of joy. Her daughter had come to her the night before and said, "Mom, we need to do a fire ceremony for Grandma. We're each going to write a letter to her, then read it while we stand around the fire. Then, we'll burn the letters and the smoke will carry our words up to heaven so when Grandma dies, she'll have letters from all of us waiting for her." The mom wrote that she knew her daughter was going to be okay. She had tools and she knew how to use them. She thanked me for everything her daughter had learned. Her daughter started school that year with much more hope, less darkness, and soon created a new group of supportive friends.

It's amazing to see the incredible impact Dancing Jaguar's Spirit Camp has on the lives of children, and even on the entire family. All of a sudden, they understand that there is a huge world inside of them that they can connect with and help keep themselves healthy, whole and peaceful.

A couple of years ago, I started receiving another message at night. This one simply stated, "The world is ready, and the children are waiting." At first, I thought I was just getting validation that I was doing a great job teaching children this body of work. After hearing the message for a couple of months, it occurred to me that maybe I should be writing all of this down and sharing it with other people to teach the children in their communities. As soon as I made that connection, I began receiving inquiries from people in other countries saying, "There's nothing like this in our country. Can you bring it to us?" Then, I knew it was time to create the Spirit Camp Teacher Training program.

"The Teacher Training" program is helping to spread Dancing Jaguar's Spirit Camp to other parts of North America, with certified Dancing Jaguar's Spirit Camp teachers throughout the US, Canada, and Mexico. With the implementation of a virtual Dancing Jaguar's Spirit Camp Teacher Training program, we can reach prospective teachers all over the world. I feel honored that I have been gifted this body of work to share with people around the world.

I feel certain that we are creating a global movement that is empowering children with a knowledge that has not typically been shared with them. It is my vision that they will grow into adults who possess a level of self-awareness and a new level of compassion and respect for themselves, their families, their communities, and the world.

Here are some things certified Spirit Camp teachers have said:

"In addition to learning the curriculum, I also experienced healing for my own inner child."

"I can't wait for you to bring this to our country."

"There aren't many things out there that I feel called to participate in. This program gives me hope because it has the ability to change the world."

If this is something you envision as well, I invite you to explore the opportunity to become a certified Spirit Camp Teacher and bring these special tools to children to carry on the message of peace, love, and joy that you hold so dear in your heart.

The world is ready, and the children are waiting.

ABOUT THE AUTHOR

EVA GOULETTE

Eva is the founder of Dancing Jaguar's Spirit Camp, a program created to teach children the importance of balance between mind, body, and spirit. To reach as many children as possible, Eva shares her specialized Spirit Camp curriculum with adults through her Spirit Camp Teacher Training Program.

Her mission is to empower and inspire the children of today so they can create the world of tomorrow, a world where all of us will thrive. She loves seeing children connect to their inner wisdom, as they discover they're connected to All That Is. Her love of children and spiritual modalities combine to empower children with hands-on training to become peaceful warriors raising the vibration and consciousness of our planet.

Eva believes the children are the ones ushering in the new Earth ~ she is simply providing the roadmap that enables them to discover their authentic self and to let their spirits soar.

Business Name: Dancing Jaguar Inspirations, LLC
Website: https://www.dancingjaguarinspirations.com/
Email: eva@dancingjaguarinspirations.com
Facebook: https://www.facebook.com/DancingJaguarsSpiritCamp

KATHERINE M. DEAN

CREATING YOUR WEALTHY DREAM LIFE & OWNING YOUR WEALTHY WOMAN WITHIN

*M*oney is Energy. Money is a gift. Money is an ebb and flow through life. Money is a tool. Pieces of paper that have created gifts for many and frustrations for others.

Throughout my 23 years in the "money business," I've found that when I speak about money, or discuss money, as a woman we speak "money" very differently. A superpower, as some may say, is having an open conversation and freedom in the discussion of money. Yes, advocating that women, in particular, be financially empowered and financially independent has a much broader perspective than just being able to take care of themselves.

Money can be the most coveted and confronting subject we face, especially as dynamic beings. So how do we have a money mindset that is aligned with our being, our purpose, our life as just a tool per se? A tool for our freedom. As a source of frustration, money can "get in the way" of things that we want to be, do or have. Money is a source of flow and freedom. It is a source for stepping into our valued contribution in the world. Being financially empowered is so much more than having millions of dollars. Being financially empowered allows women to be able to value their expertise, value their worth, and share with others, so they themselves value their own purpose and goals. Women as a whole are an incredible energy. I am you, and you are me. So I ask you, why, when it comes to the subject of money, do we hold ourselves back? Avoid discussing opportunities or collaborate to create more money flow in our lives. How is it that we still get 82c on the dollar for our services? This is an exchange that energetically is imbalanced.

In this chapter, I will share with you tools, tips, ideas, suggestions, and experiences to Own Your Worth and the power of choice. My hope is that you share this with others, and together we can create a more awakened Wealthy Woman Within all of us.

At the age of 33, I was living the "American Dream". Perfect house, white picket fence, two healthy young daughters, a golden retriever, a successful career, and life was good. Not perfect, but in my early thirties, what more can you ask for. It was the way I had pictured my life being since my mid-20s. I also wished for more and had bigger dreams, sometimes past the extent of what was right in front of me. Until a Tuesday in May 2010, when my "perfect life" was completely derailed. My partner in life decided our relationship was over. Financially I was falling apart. My income wouldn't sustain the family home. I became a single mom to my 1 & 3 year old daughters, and this was not in "my plan." Not only was my life of rocking my grandchildren on the front porch ripped out from underneath me, but the financial rug was ripped out from beneath me. My dreams and goals and everything I knew for the future were not possible. I thought of myself as a failure… a statistic. My life as I knew it was going to be gone! The life I had poured my hopes, dreams, and future into was now a thing of the past.

The fact was, I was disheartened with life, and thinking about a hopeful future that would be fulfilling wasn't in my view. That exciting, successful, fulfilling future was very overwhelming and nowhere within reach. My life, my bright future had been pulled apart, I felt like a complete failure. In fact, how could I have put all this effort and energy into one person, one relationship, and yet I was so naïve that it was all falling apart? The trajectory of my life as

I had always dreamed, envisioned, was torn away from me on that Tuesday Date Night in May 2010. The words abundance, light, joy, and energy were a thing of the past. After living in this state of being for six months, and my left eye twitching for what may have seemed like an eternity—walking around like a zombie. One day I had my "oh shit" moment! We all have them when life or a moment smacks you so hard that you'll never be able to unsee it! I was playing with my adorable young daughters and was watching them —full of hope, dreams, and future and unscathed by LIFE. I made the decision that I would never have the FINANCIAL RUG RIPPED OUT FROM UNDERNEATH ME AGAIN. It was that defining moment that changed the trajectory of my life forever. It's the moment when I discovered my life's purpose, to empower One Million women with financial freedom. I didn't know the actions to take or even who would listen to me, but I knew women needed to Own Their Worth and Live Their Worth in order for the financial trajectory of women to change their lives. How could I be the one that changed my future? I was a failure at marriage, a disappointment to my family, and working for an employer that completely undervalued my expertise? My greatest failure in life turned into my driving force! The commitment to see my daughters would no longer grow up in a .82c on the dollar income world, and women would step into their power, realize their self-worth and shift the future became the story I would share. Today, in 2021, I've shared these tools and ideas with over 50,000 women through speaking events, podcasts, emails, social media, and being a Financial Advisor and CERTIFIED FINANCIAL PLANNER™.

To speak all things money, we first have to understand our relationship with money. We often derive our money beliefs from who we were raised. Good, bad, indifferent; the money conversation usually isn't the easiest one, but there are many ways to make it easier, and I'm going to share them with you today. If you think back to how you were raised and the household money beliefs, can you see how you may be living in the same patterns? What I'm sharing with you today are habits, beliefs, and ideas to get super comfortable with the money conversation. Why, you may ask?

Money is Energy
Money is an ebb and flow
Money is an accessibility
Money is Freedom
Money is an Easy Breezy Retirement
Money is Contribution
Money is Peace of Mind
Money makes life easier
Money is a Legacy
Money is just a tool

There is a direct correlation between money, self-worth, confidence, valuing yourself, following your dreams, living your greatest potential, and your limitless Self. Money is a necessity and a form of exchange. Now, I know when I speak of it from this perspective, you may feel lots of emotion coming up. Let those emotions come up, write them down, know that all of this is your relationship with money, and at any time, that relationship can be mended or transformed. The flip side to your relationship is that money is also a necessity for living. It ranks right up there with food, water, and shelter. It's a form of exchange for activities and items that bring us joy in life, traveling, a new pair of boots, crystals, supporting our children's activities, enjoying a nice dinner out. I could go on with my happy list… but when we consider money as just a tool or a piece of paper and as a form of exchange, it takes a lot of emotion out of the equation. It takes the good versus evil, restraints, and low energy out of money. Here's where it gets fun, how can we have a better relationship with money to create the life, possibly even the legacy we want to leave behind.

First, we have to get really clear on our money mindset and the energy that follows behind that. Money is a powerful energy source, and no matter how "hard" you try to build a business, create wealth, increase your income or pay off debt if you and money aren't in a good relationship, this energy is going to foul up your goals and dreams for your life.

Second, we need to know our spending habits. For instance, are we spending because we are sad, angry, upset, or are we spending money because it brings us joy.

Third, are we saying one thing and doing another. I'm sure you've all been there like I have, you say you want to be debt-free, but you continue to spend money with credit cards. You're really looking forward to that trip that may cost $5000, but you're not in action to put those funds away, so that trip never happens. I've been there. I was speaking into existence a life and dreams for someone else because my actions behind my goals weren't creating my reality. Again, the energy isn't going to flow where the actions don't go.

Let my trials and failures steer you in the direction of where your future is headed. 1998 was the first time I stepped into my financial services career, right out of college, naïve, whimsical, and full of hope. My dreams of becoming a Millionaire by 40 to create an easier life for myself seemed lightyears ahead of me. I was ignorant and influenced. I was influenced by friends and family and influenced by social media and the "wants" that really didn't serve me. Expensive purses, a car payment too high, lots of nights out drinking with my friends, interest on credit cards that I would someday pay off, student loans, price tags I couldn't really afford. I share this because these are the exact things that kept me from achieving Millionaire status by the time I turned 40. But, that Tuesday in May 2010 was the kick in the ass I needed to know that my trajectory for my life wasn't on track. I was in my early 30s and wasn't even close to being on track to be a Millionaire. You may ask, why was that so important? I knew if I could get there, I'd be able to help others create their dreams and goals and to be able to become the philanthropist I wanted to be, donate to causes that were near and dear to my heart, and have the freedom I wanted to travel the world. What happened in May 2010 was a defining moment in my life. It was my adulting moment when I realized that I had to take Radical Responsibility for my life. What I create in my life, the goals I set, the actions I take, the accomplishments and success are 100% my responsibility—to be clear not all the goals and aspirations I have are financial. Like all of you, I have dreams of traveling, contributing to causes, being able to pick up and go whenever I'd like to, have a tiny home on a huge piece of unscathed land with a lake in the distance, maybe a treehouse because that seems cooler and creating a legacy that not only my daughters will inherit but my grandchildren and great-grandchildren. And at age 44, I became a Millionaire. The Millionaire my mother always wanted me to marry.

The beauty of life is that we all are miracles put on this earth. To fulfill our potential and be the beacon for others to fulfill their greatness. We all have the power within ourselves to live a life of alignment, ease, and flow. The Wealthy Woman Within is the person we need to bring to the forefront to create our dream life. Never underestimate the power of an incredible Why and Vision for yourself because that is where the magic happens. Magic and miracles happen on the other side of fear, discouragement, naysayers, and limiting beliefs. So I ask you, as you are reading this chapter, what is it that you are holding yourself from, and what dreams and goals do you think about daily that are being held inside of you? The gift that was meant to be shared with the world? And since I talk money, let's talk about what is holding you back from creating the income and becoming the Millionaire you deserve to be?

Money habits are the key to creating the financial life you want to live. Saving, investing, paying off debt, living below your means, utilizing your company's retirement plan, increasing your prices as a business owner, owning your worth, and taking small actions over time will begin to create the successful money habits necessary to achieve the financial freedom you deserve.

Small actions over time lead to big results. This is what got me back on track after financially falling on my ass and becoming a single mom. Although 40 seemed like an eternity in 1998, it snuck up on me very quickly, and not to mention, life happens. We have to zig when we want to zag, but having the vision and our why in place will allow us to have flexibility. It's when the vision and the why are missing when we can get easily derailed from our future Self. Putting a plan in place with our money and having our money work for us versus us working for money is what Albert Einstein said was the eighth wonder of the world. Here's the deal, money over time that is working for you compounds, and $1.00 today may be $10 in a few years. We need to work smarter with our money to create the dream life we've always thought about. There are simple and complex ways to have our money working for us. If we just get our own hard-earned cash working for us, it's like getting a pay raise. Our money is working just as hard as we do, and eventually, that pays off. For instance, using a compounding calculator as a hypothetical. Think about if you save $100.00 per week for 30 years at 10% interest, you would have contributed a total of $150,100.00 but have an investment value of $991,446.05. This is the power of compounding! That is why you often hear the sooner you save, the more money you will have. This is the power of our money working for us. This is what got me back on track after I was derailed, and the dream of becoming a Millionaire was way too far in the future. Let's also think about how that money working for us would create ease in our lives.

Failing fast in a venture is one of the greatest lessons I've learned for financial freedom. Have you ever focused on a passion project, invested in a business that wasn't working? Spent hours and hours doing something that wasn't giving you a return on your investment? With this example, I'm not focusing on hobbies. I love to garden and would consider myself an amateur photographer, but those are hobbies. I can spend hours chasing sunrises and sunsets, but my intention is to share those gifts with others on social media without monetizing. Failing fast in a business or idea is another necessary tool with taking radical responsibility for your financial future, and let's face it, no one likes to fail. But allowing yourself to fail always comes with an incredible lesson. It allows us to evaluate what may have gone wrong, what not to do in the future, and pivots the direction of our dream life.

Creating multiple streams of income is a way to bulletproof yourself from financial downturns. In this economy, multiple streams of income could be investing in real estate, residuals from being an author, actor, online programs, silent investor in someone else's business for-profits, network marketing, and referral income, just to name a few. I'm an advocate of multiple streams of income when you're in a steady state with one stream of income. What do I mean by that? If you are open and in conversation, there will be many opportunities that come your way, and not all of them are appropriate for your growth and your future. Know which businesses and investments are making money. Make sure you're creating income before diversifying your multiple streams of income. This is also where I'd be your advocate to have the right advisors around you so you can make the best decision for yourself based on your entire financial life.

Be the Chief Financial Officer of your life. Although this may sound like a very big, and at times, overwhelming job, the fact is no one but you can focus and create the goals that you are looking to achieve. So it's important that we understand what it will take to create a financial goal in our lives, how long it will take, and what actions steps are needed to achieve our goals. Of course, keep your advisors that have come before you that have had success getting to their goals too. To take radical responsibility for your financial life, your habits will have to change because what got you here won't get you where you're going. A few action steps I share with clients is to know your true financial picture. For instance, list all your debts, income streams, monthly, quarterly and annual bills, and get really clear on your financial picture. Take some time and write down the action steps that got you where you are today. Decide, because everything in life happens when you decide and declare new goals. Where do you want to be in 10 years, 5 years, 3 years, and 1 year from today? Throughout my years of "working with money" and helping incredible people just like you to set goals, how much can really be done when you have your action plan in 1 year! Imagine what you can accomplish in 10 years!

There is a secret behind having successful money habits. Be crystal clear on the goals that you want to achieve. Intention and energy flow within your daily thoughts and your mindset. If you have a slight doubt that you cannot create financial freedom in your life, you are going to face obstacles. Financial confidence, a healthy relationship with money, and a plan to get you there with mini goals along the way are the secret sauce. The money conversation can seem complicated. Confronting and confusing with fancy words and algorithms, That is exactly what it is; jargon.

Keep your dreams and vision in front of you daily, check in with your goals monthly and start to see how your future will begin to unfold in the most beautiful way.

You are worth it! You were meant to be The Wealthy Woman Within.

"Let the alignment (with Well-Being) be the first and foremost,
and let everything else be secondary
and not only will you have an eternally joyous journey,
but everything you ever imagined will
flow effortlessly into your experience.
There is nothing you cannot be or do or have –
But your dominant intent is to be Joyful.
The doing and having will come into alignment
Once you get that down."
-Abraham Hicks

ABOUT THE AUTHOR

KATHERINE M. DEAN

Katherine M. Dean, Mom, Dog Mom, Wife, Entrepreneur, Author, CERTIFIED FINANCIAL PLANNER™, Owner of Living Your Worth, Inc, & EMALS Holding Corp.

Katherine is known as "The Wealthy Woman Within," as her experience in the financial industry has helped hundreds of business owners, individuals, couples and women create their path to financial freedom. She has spent over 20 years guiding people with their financial goals and supporting them to be the CFO of their own lives. Katherine is also an advocate women's equal pay, women owning their worth while being their most powerful and authentic Self.

Women owning their power and uniqueness, standing in their true authentic self, unapologetically are the most powerful women in the world! Never apologize for the woman you know in your soul you were meant to be!

Create your Wealthy Dream Life.

Let's connect on Social & Contact Information
Cell: 914-649-4413
Email: Katherine@katherindeanbrands.com
Instagram: @thewealthywomanwithin
Facebook: https://www.facebook.com/KatherineMaryDean
LinkedIn: https://www.linkedin.com/in/katherine-dean-cfp%C2%AE-a0072679/

Website: https://opalwealthadvisors.com/working-with-us/opalwomen/

SHANNON A. FISHER

THE PERFECT STORM: TRUSTING WHAT IS ALREADY WITHIN YOU

I remember hearing my body say. "Shannon, you need to find a new pace in life."

What, now? No way, I can't; there is too much going on. What if they find out?

This was me in 2018.

I had just finished an exhausting and tiring business season where I was doing everything in my power to keep things afloat while traveling everywhere, rushing home never to miss kids' events, and pushing the envelope way beyond my capacity.

A few years prior, I had felt like I needed a change. Lots of entrepreneurs get bored at a certain part of their journey; we love to be creative. However, I was so bound to my business that I was scared to make any waves. In all reality, I started to hide from my truth. I didn't want to acknowledge what was going on and how out of alignment physically, mentally, and spiritually I had become. I wasn't happy, struggling to make sense of it all and running my poor body into the ground. I had been caught up in a belief that something has to be sacrificed to "have it all" in life. I've seen this play out in almost all successful books for high performers and had been internalizing this in a way that I didn't even notice until it was almost too late.

I had climbed the mountain of success; we had it all. However, amidst my journey, I knew well enough that I didn't want to reach the state of being successful only to either lose it all or become grumpy and dissatisfied. I studied, worked on myself to become a great leader, and "thought" I was leading myself well and doing all the things shown before to reach this pinnacle state of success.

But something just wasn't right.

I was so unhappy and lost, and many nights, I wondered what the heck was this all for?

I should be so grateful; I should be happy… right?

I couldn't go back to who I was before as that woman didn't have the financial success that we had come to rely on. Yet, I was getting signals from my body that told me that I needed to create a new PACE in life. With three kids ages 7,8,9, and two businesses running, I was struggling to keep my head above water—I chose the lane of "suck it up buttercup" "put your big girl panties on and move forward."

THE RIP CURRENT.

Have you ever seen the warnings about the rip current? You know the black flags you see near the ocean advising you NOT to go swimming. Precautionary notices state that if you are caught in one to don't swim against the current, relax and float, and however, even the best swimmers can get swept away from shore.

In fact, 47 people lose their lives each year for being caught in a rip current. A rip current is fast-moving water that pulls objects, including people, out to sea.

This was me. I was a great swimmer in both life and business; however, this rip current got the better of me. The worst thing was,

I knew I was in one, but I kept swimming against the current, and I was getting exhausted. I was drifting further and further away from shore, and I was losing the battle quickly.

TIDES ARE CHANGING.

July 2018 was the beginning of our beautiful family vacation, four weeks to unwind and see Canada's East Coast. I had just finished my intense traveling schedule, assisting leaders in growing their health and wellness business and doing lots of speaking gigs. The worst thing was I wasn't feeling good, bouts of dizziness, weight gain with no reason, and I was so exhausted. I would have moments of feeling like I was drowning or pulled under the water like a rip current in the ocean.

These 4-weeks were the beginning of a massive unravelling of my life.

We arrived at the Bay of Fundy, home to one of the world's most extreme tidal movements in the world. I was so excited to see the iconic landmasses in the water as we stepped out on the ocean floor. Our whole family was in sheer amazement as we ran along the bottom, looking for whatever was left behind from the last tide that had come in.

I remember walking and seeing the red earth under my feet and feeling so connected and clear in those moments—all of life seemed to make sense.

Soon, it would be covered again with water, only to reappear a few hours later. I was fascinated with this—the rolling of the tides and how our beautiful moon controls it all.

I knew something big was changing for me. I was scared and also calm and connected. If I only knew what was going to happen next…

How often are we caught with that thought? "If I only knew," the truth is we probably would never truly know our greatness if we had a crystal ball. The resilience and grit we develop by flowing through life and learning the lessons along the way. It truly is a journey.

A few days before, my walk on the ocean floor was pretty rough. I was quite sick and was feeling dizzy. I had these moments before that felt like I had sea legs or was just in an elevator. It was like being on a rollercoaster and never ever getting off, or like being tossed around in a lifeboat crashing against the shore. I would grab my head to just "stop the spin." Sometimes it felt like a tidal wave flowing over me, but these days were worse. I thought that maybe I had picked up the "flu", but no one else got sick. Intense body pain, fever, chills, and shaking at night were uncontrollable. This wasn't the first time I had intense body shakes; they had plagued me on and off for years—but never this intense.

I did like what I have always done; burnt some incense, took more vitamins, packed down some Advil, got a bit of rest, powered up, and moved forward. This was our family vacation, and I wasn't going to allow myself to be sick to stop it.

As the summer went on, I knew something wasn't right.

Early in September, the kids had just gone back to school, and I was about to begin my next season in business. Then it hit me, "Houston, we have a problem." Two massively large lumps grew literally overnight in my groin. I was scared—Chris was away, and I didn't know what to do. Finally, I surrendered and went to the hospital.

"Maybe it's viral," said the doctor. "It should clear up in a few days."

I was scared, I didn't know what was going on, my business was amid a massive market correction, and I couldn't support it. I couldn't sacrifice anything else, and quickly, my identity was shifting.

I had hope, but over the next few weeks, things got worse. The hardest part was that my traditional medical doctors kept telling me that I was "fine," extraordinarily healthy and that it was all in my head. "FINE" was not a term to describe my intense pain or evenings when I couldn't even get out of bed to kiss my kid's goodnight. I felt 100 years old, living in a 39-year-old body. I cried and shook myself to sleep many nights and wondered if I'd ever feel healthy again.

In the spring of 2019, things got even worse, and I was starting to feel like something may be seriously wrong and that I may die. They tested me for everything from cancer, MS, Lupus, Malaria, HIV, all of it. Nothing, again, nothing was found!! Some blood work was off, but my doctor and other traditional MDs couldn't figure it out.

The scariest moment was when I started to lose my words and thoughts. I couldn't write, and speaking was becoming more and more difficult. I remember saying, please just don't take my brain. This part of me is the one thing I need to feel like I can live and contribute to the world. I remember sitting down at my computer and trying to write; nothing would come out. The brain fog was intense, and I couldn't finish sentences. My husband and kids wondered what on earth I was trying to say. This devastated me.

I was losing the battle quickly, and I needed answers; I had to heal.
I was in a rip current and couldn't swim out.
I was so exhausted; I couldn't keep going any longer.

My life was crashing around me. I was losing it all, and for the first time ever, I didn't care. I just wanted to live.

The only thing I had left to choose was to surrender to the current, and I decided to float vs. sink.

I remember asking myself, what on earth was I doing? What needed to change?

Amidst this storm, I realized that this rip current was just setting me out to sea to live into another pace and facilitated one of the greatest lessons of allowing, forgiving, and just being.

SELF ADVOCACY: TIME TO CAPTAIN UP!!

High Tide Lifts all Ships.

While I was in the storm of my dis-ease, I noticed a t-shirt I was wearing, and it said, "be fearless," and it changed everything. These simple words started me back on my journey to my next level of greatness. This became my motto, and then I saw another acronym for fear. "To Face Everything And Rise" Yes, I thought to myself—time to rise. High tides raise all ships.

I looked about my life and wrote out the steps that I had done before that had got me out of fast-moving waters; RISE kept coming to me. Then, I broke it down. Reflect, Innovate, Strategize and Execute. These were the steps I had taken time and time before to chart a new course or direction in my life, but this time I need to go even deeper in my journey.

Part of my process has been that each year I choose a word that acts as a lighthouse for me. It helps me with staying the course and in making decisions. For a large part of my life, that word was very focused on my business endeavours, and occasionally it would impact other parts of my life. I would teach others to make sure that it was a well-rounded wheel of life while I still was tied to this addiction of sacrifice and suffering.

In 2019, I realized that I needed to shift to a "wholeness" way of being to truly heal. No more going part of the way, in the past when I started to feel better and then stop doing what I was doing to get the results. I needed to become the captain of my own leadership and wellbeing. I had to choose to go ALL IN. The word in 2019 was Results. In 2020 it was Pace, and now in 2021, it's Access.

Results: I set affirmations that I would get the results to start my healing journey.

As I set my intention and affirmation to heal and get answers, I remember standing in my kitchen, asking myself some powerful questions. "Shannon, be resourceful. The answer is within you." My body felt hijacked, something else was running the show, and I knew the answers were within me. When I quieted my mind and was just standing with a solid intention for it to flow out of me, it happened. LYME, Shannon, it's Lyme disease. It was like; a lightning bolt ran through me.

At that moment, life made perfect sense. My mom had Lyme before she was pregnant with me, and instantly, I felt connected back to my soul and the powerful intuition of my body. I was becoming clear again and clearing out the chaos. Now, I sought confirmation and a plan to heal.

I had learned for years about the power of meditation and allowing my intuition to guide me. However, through the years of "believing" I needed to be sacrificing shit to get to where I thought I wanted to be, I had been lowering that light and vibration.

I realized that if I did my internal work, I would be more aware of the team that I needed to attract to support me. Since my western medical team couldn't help me heal, I didn't allow that to stop me.

How often are you told by someone else, "no", "move on", "you're okay"; but you know in your heart and soul you are not, or that you deserve more? In life, I've learned to not always listen to others but to truly follow my heart. If I wanted a different outcome, it was going to be up to me to figure this one out.

The team. One of my life lessons has been the team that gets you to one place in life isn't the same team that can get you to the next level in your life. Surrounding myself by an all-star team and meant the difference between leading well or just surviving.

So, I went on a quest to find a new wellness team; every captain is only as great as their crew. I've always believed that there are so many great practitioners or business partners in the world; my job is to find the ones that work with me. I kept asking and advocating for my health, and I created an A-Team of both Functional medicine doctors and traditional doctors. What they offered me was **teamwork and hope.**

The week before I turned 40, I got my result, confirming my disease; it's Lyme.

Question:
Who is a part of your All-star winning team to support you in reaching your next level of greatness?

MY LIGHTHOUSE MOMENTS. FAITH FORWARD.

You may have heard of failing forward in life, but there was a more profound lesson for me than failing forward; it was having **faith forward. Faith forward allows me to have my own inner lighthouse on.** Shining bright for me to guide myself to my next step, next adventure—it's my inner compass. It is the ACCESS point to my higher self and my learning of God's grace and purpose for me here on earth.

It hasn't always been this way.

A few years ago, I started to see others in my inner circle have a deeper level of success than I was having. There was a deeper level of understanding, joy, and peace that was running through them. To say I was envious would be a lie. What I started to understand was that they had unwavering faith. Some preached it; others didn't; however, there was an energy around them that drew me in, and I wanted it.

I've read many spiritual books, the bible from time to time, and it was enough to get by, however this time I felt like there was so much more I had to learn and lean into and that there was a big void in my soul that required profound discovery.

Like every high achiever, I went on a quest again. The last time I did this, I was young, trying to understand more of my humanity. To be honest, I wanted to understand more of my greatness and potential as it is the only thing that haunts me in life— to die without fully expressing what I am here to do on earth.

Even with this feeling of not living into full expression, I felt the resistance to lean in. It wasn't until my dis-ease got the best of me and I had to turn to the only part of me that was left standing.

This journey has not been one of being struck by lightning but more of a vision of light off in the distance guiding me back to safety and hope. Over the past three years, the light has become brighter and brighter and to the point where I could no longer ignore it. When you are sick and have what appears to be an invisible disease, you start to learn about anything that will give you courage, strength, and support. For me, I had to sink or at least feel like I was before I was really ready just to follow the light.

The more I resisted, the more complex the storm was. The more I leaned into the light, the easier it was to get back on my feet and chart a new course.

Hope and faith were my way home. I trusted the process and finally truly believed in my spiritual guide and that he was always there to guide me when I'm lost. **This was my lighthouse moment.**

One of my biggest shifts has to finally call God "God" unapologetically. I used to change my language to suit the people around me. As I committed to just claiming my voice, I've come into more alignment each day.

I realize that the way to the true love of self and see my soul and me for what it is. Unbound, untethered and free.

Free to have faith and do it anyway. To live large, to disrupt the normal, and seek the truth from within. Faith forward has given me the access point to live into my zone of genius and to say "no" to the Good so that I can say a YES to the GREAT that's coming my way!!

QUESTION:

How would you rate your level of trusting your faith? When was the last time you spent nurturing your soul and spiritual wellness?

What lighthouse moments have you had in your life? How did you get safely to shore?

TO WEATHER ALL STORMS.

When you live through a storm, you start to realize that another one will always come. The question is not if, but when. Knowing this puts my heart at ease, for I had run from the feelings of pain and loss in the past. Now, I know to prepare for the storm.

Being prepared for the next storm has opened the gates for me to live into a new way of being that is truly aligned and allows me to access my inner leadership in a way that brings out the best in me so that I can serve those around me.

To gain more wisdom, I now choose to live with more flexibility and adaptability. I've had to work on surrendering, releasing, and unhooking myself from masculine energy of sacrifice and struggle to what I refer to now as my "And too" feminine energy. "And too" is about truly having it all. It's about having fantastic health AND a fantastic family, career, finances, relationships. It's having both, not just "this or that." This is my way to live into my own peak performance in life.

Living into healthy boundaries of my life and expectations of myself and others, a simplified and aligned vision, and taking consistent action. I choose to take 100% responsibility for everything IN and NOT in my life. It's about trusting when I need to pause and rest and not feel guilty for doing it.

Through this past storm, I realized that I was charting a new course in my life and that in order for me to truly cross over, I had to keep moving with the storm and look to the lighthouse for guidance and protection.

CHOOSING TO BECOME LIGHTHOUSE LEADER.

Through my journey, I realized that we all could get taken out to sea, like a boat leaving the dock on its maiden voyage. At some point, we lose our perspective of where the lighthouse is, and we need to lean into our plan and trust the process. Through the ups and downs, we continue to move forward.

Becoming a lighthouse leader allows me to support those who are in the midst of the storm to create new plans and do the work required to arrive safely. It's not about smooth sailing, as we all have to weather our own storms but more of providing light in the distance, so you have hope and courage to keep going.

By living with complete intention and having faith forward now allows me to stay calm in the midst of a storm.

Are you feeling called to lead more in your life? I can only encourage you to choose to be a lighthouse leader, one that weathers the storms but stays a beacon of light and hope for the people around you. You never know how shining light bright could be the difference between someone sinking or surviving.

If you get caught in a rip current, surrender to the process, breathe and allow the transformation of something great to happen in your life. On your way back to shore, know that there will be moments when you may feel like it's hard, that you may not get there, but keep your head up for someone will be in the lighthouse providing you with the light and hope you need.

That will be your reminder to trust, trust the light within you and keep going.

Keep the light on, my friend.

ABOUT THE AUTHOR

SHANNON A. FISHER

Shannon A. Fisher is a successful wholistic entrepreneur, passionate speaker, and business mentor.

She has dedicated her life to empowering women to lead themselves well in life and business, to claim their voice, face the fear and rise, and become the master steward of their leadership.

She has been in the wellness and leadership industry for the past 20+ years. Her continual thirst for seeking the truth has lead her to become a lifelong learner of health, leadership, and human behaviour. This knowledge and wisdom have served and empowered her clients in achieving extraordinary success throughout the years.

Shannon feels that her most significant achievement to date is her family. Married to her husband Chris and with their three children, they continue to embrace a growth-based mindset. The words "Strength of Griffin. Grace of love. Wisdom of Gabriel" are tattooed on her arm that explains the qualities of her children, her earthly guides.

Born and raised in Ontario, Canada, this mogul mom loves to be in nature and be surrounded by her family, friends and pets.

Check out Shannon's work below to discover your next level of greatness.
website: www.shannonafisher.com

Facebook: @befearlesswithshannon
IG: @shannon.a.fisher

Launching in the fall of 2021 - Pillars of Light Candle Company
Bringing more love and light to your home and the world.
Join the movement.
www.pillarsoflight.co

TIFFANY MCCOY

MARKETING WITH HEART: HOW MY INTUITION BROUGHT ME EXACTLY WHERE I NEEDED TO BE

The summer of 2006 was a very happy time for me. I was in my early 20s—going to college, working, riding motorcycles, and having fun with my friends. As summer approached, a good friend invited me to go on a long ride with some other friends to a small mountain town about three hours from home. Initially, I agreed to go, but as the day of the trip approached, I started feeling less sure. I almost decided to cancel when a voice inside me SCREAMED at me that I needed to go on this ride because something was going to happen. At the time, I thought nothing of it —I didn't even know what intuition was at that point in my life- but decided I should go on the ride.

About halfway to our destination, in a location without cell service or even homes or businesses, my friend was in a horrific accident which required a life flight to the hospital, weeks in a medically induced coma in the ICU, and resulted in a traumatic brain injury, several broken bones, and many other very serious injuries.

That was my first conscious experience with my intuition; although I didn't understand what it was at the time, it had scared me. I shut it out, not knowing how powerful of a tool it would be for my life.

After this accident, my life began shifting course. I got a new job. Then another. I moved and adopted a dog. To me, it was just a normal 20 something life changes—but I see now that I was pivoting and realigning with myself again and again along my path.

Fast forward to 2012. I had just given birth to my daughter. As I lay there looking at her, I had this experience of time standing still. It seemed as if the universe was opening in front of me and this overwhelming sense that everything in my life was transforming, not because of the baby, but because of who I was now, having stepped through the portal into motherhood. I had what can best be described as a vision—although it was not in pictures, but rather a complete and visceral knowing in every fiber of my being that radically shifted the trajectory of my life. It was a knowing that I was the creator I had been searching for. That I could create anything, I wanted in my life. That nothing I could imagine was outside the realm of possibility.

This experience was the catalyst for the next several years of exploration into my intuition. I started reading everything I could get my hands on—at that time, there wasn't close to the volume of spiritually focused literature that we can find today. I began to understand that what I was searching for was an understanding of my intuition, the Law of Attraction, and how my own inner knowing could guide me without fail.

I spent a year with a spiritual mentor and became a Reiki Master. As my self-practice became strong, I began to recognize all the points in my life where I would be moving in one direction only to wake up the next day and do a complete 180 shift in another direction. These pivots, I began to understand, were guiding me toward where I am today and where I am going.

Every pivot was a realignment to my true north. It was my intuition calling me home.

My next big pivot came in late 2019. I had been making soap as a hobby for a little while and was really getting into it. I decided to join some local seasonal markets to sell my soaps. I paid registration fees and made an inventory to start attending these local markets.

One day, I woke up and knew that this was not in alignment for me anymore. I decided to forfeit my entrance fee's to the upcoming spring shows, and I quit making soap. A few months later, COVID hit, and my state was completely shut down—essentially destroying the local seasonal market economy.

So many times, I felt alone and unsupported when I would make a big shift. I see now that each shift was another opportunity for me to believe in myself. The more inner work I did, the easier the pivots would come, and the more "on track" I would feel.

I was labeled multi-passionate, which helped other people understand me. But that has never been really true for me. I find things that I am interested in, and I go 100 miles an hour in the direction of that thing, learn what I need to learn, and move on to the next thing. Once I lost interest, it was impossible for me to recommit, and I would once again pivot to the next thing. As a child, this meant changing activities and hobbies. As an adult, this meant changing jobs—anything from retail to long haul truck driving to office desk jobs, nothing was off the table.

I've never thought of myself as being truly multi-passionate. I was just following myself... following my intuition, led by an invisible string, to exactly where I need to be. I didn't always understand that it was my intuition guiding me, but as I learned to connect deeply with myself, it became clear that that is exactly what had been showing me the way.

Through every shift, big or small, one thing remained constant—my need to connect with people in a meaningful way. No matter where I am or what I'm doing, I find that I am driven by the need to connect and understand people. What motivates them, what inspires them. Their hopes and dreams and fears. And no matter what, I always want to help them.

I am a natural caregiver. Even as a child, I was always saving worms from puddles or bringing home stray cats and kittens. Motherhood came to me, as second nature as breathing, giving me the chance to find my voice as I stepped into this new role.

That innate desire to help lead me to try out coaching for a bit. I learned pretty quickly that I didn't want to be a coach... mainly because I could not get behind the marketing trends at the time. The focus of marketing being pushed at the time was to make people feel bad so that they will buy your widget and bobble to "solve their problem." This style of marketing is still being promoted today, but I was fortunate to never get on board. When I realized I couldn't market myself, I knew I had to quit wasting time on something that would never go where I wanted to go.

I transitioned to virtual assisting, a skill that is natural and easy for me. I loved the work and found that it was filling my desire for connection. Slowly I once again began to grow disheartened by what I saw as cheap marketing gimmicks and questionable practices in the industries I was supporting.

I couldn't get behind the fear-mongering, salt in the wound & fake urgency tactics that the vast majority of people were using to market their offering to people they claimed to care about. I knew I couldn't be a part of a culture built on hurting people and manipulating them into buying a product that was 80% fluff while claiming it would solve all their problems.

My intuition was screaming at me to find a different way. This time I recognized the voice, and it was easy to listen to. I could see that there was another way—a way to market that stems from connection, trust, and a genuine desire to help. I still didn't know what that way looked like, but I knew that if I could imagine it, it was possible.

This time, pivoting wasn't as easy for me—I didn't know where I was going, but I was already off the boat. I had to lean into myself, my inner knowing, and trust that I could find what I was looking for.

Fairly quickly, I did just that, even though I didn't know it at the time.

I had applied for a job and didn't get even a callback—but that job application sparked in me an unrelenting desire to take a deep dive into marketing. This felt pretty crazy at the time because I hated marketing and everything that "marketing" meant to me. After all, it had nothing but negative connotations in my mind.

After a few weeks of being completely stuck on the idea that I had to take a deep dive into marketing, I found just the thing I had been looking for without ever knowing I was seeking it. I found a company that was teaching marketing in a completely different way. A way that focused on understanding people, connecting with them, and from that place creating offers to solve real and urgent problems for their clients.

I have completely immersed myself in this new way of relating to people in the online market space. I was quickly learning everything I possibly could. I felt as though I had finally found my voice. I had finally found a way to connect with people and to help others connect without making anyone feel bad in the process.

My intuition had guided me to the perfect place at the perfect time to find exactly what I was looking for, realigning me with my true north once again.

As I leaned into the training, I began to develop an entirely new appreciation for marketing as a spiritual practice—a practice that focuses on connection, understanding, and appreciation to bring people to the next level on their own journeys.

I used what I learned and paired it with my own spiritual knowledge to begin offering marketing services for other entrepreneurs in an entirely new way. Instead of focusing on the pain and lack mentality of traditional methods—I help take dream clients on a journey to discover the greater possibilities for their lives.

I use marketing paired with my own inner knowing as a tool to bring people hope, fill their hearts with passion and inspire them to take action to make positive changes in their own lives. This becomes a bridge of connection with people everywhere and anywhere. It's an opportunity to positively impact people's lives, not just make another sale.

Every step of the way, my intuition has guided me. Every time I saw a need for change, that inner voice was there. Every time I pivoted, that voice was there. Every time I felt like I had no idea what the next right step was, that voice was there.

I love to connect with myself in the moment, feeling into my heart space, slowing down, and then once I'm connected, I ask my question. I'd like to share with you an exercise that I do when I'm working, and I need to get clear on the next right step:

Take a nice deep breath in through your nose and out through your mouth.
Take three more nice slow breaths and turn your focus inward.
Imagining you are surrounded by a warm golden light.
Feel into your heart space.
Notice, without judgment, how it feels now - Are you contracted? Are you expansive?
Take three more nice slow breaths, focusing on your heart space.
On your last exhale, ask yourself your question.
Now just sit quietly and listen or feel for any answers.
When you are ready, thank your inner knowing for supporting you, and let go.

You may get an answer right away, or you may not. I find that I get the best answers when I give myself some space from the task at hand to actually think. Going for a walk, doing the dishes, driving, or taking a shower are some of the ways that I find useful to tap into my intuition when I'm trying to solve a work-related—or really any —problem.

In early 2021 I had my most powerful pivot yet. I woke up one morning with a deep sense of understanding that I was doing exactly what I was trying to avoid doing. I was working—trading dollars for hours—telling myself that I was doing this so I could be with my kids and do something fulfilling for myself. However, in reality, I was just leaving myself stressed and overwhelmed with too many balls in the air every day.

I found that I couldn't show up the way I wanted to anywhere with the current model I existed in. Leaning into that knowing and opening my heart to other possibilities lead me to shift my entire business model and make another major chang—refocusing on the things that are most important to me.

Every time I listen to my intuition and make a pivot in my life, it gets easier. I find it easier to see the signs and guideposts early— before I burn out and become overwhelmed. Listening to my intuition earlier allows me to shift with ease rather than shifting from a place of panic and fear.

Instead of reacting, I allow myself to be lead along the path of ease and joy.

Knowing this has allowed me to shift into a business model that is sustainable and divinely supported. It has led me to shift into marketing with heart.

ABOUT THE AUTHOR

TIFFANY MCCOY

Tiffany McCoy is the founder of Virtually Tiffany, a digital marketing support service offering Done For You Sales Funnels, Launch Planning and Management, and Digital Course Development for Spiritual Entrepreneurs. As a certified Master Marketer, her skills include strategy, planning, and content creation for the online space. She is an expert at Marketing with Heart - using marketing as a tool for connection and empowerment.

Tiffany lives with her family and their 4 dogs in the beautiful state of Washington. She enjoys gardening, exploring, and reading good books. She loves to learn and is always trying something new.

Website: https://tiffanymccoy.co/
Email: hello@virtuallytiffany.co

ELISSA NAUMAN

AWAKENING 2.0

I was not always conscious of the affinity between nature and spirituality. As a child, I loved to play outdoors in the woods or at the beach but I took flowers, plants, trees, and the ocean for granted, not fully respecting what they offer. As a young adult, I barely regarded any synchrony between the earth and humans; I viewed us merely as inhabitants. Today, I embody the connection that I have with the earth, knowing that she provides everything that I need to live a long, healthy, and happy life.

I credit this revelation to my progressive journey of uncovering my life's purpose, which began around the time I was 27. At that time, I became aware of a little voice in my head that kept nagging me to "do more." I knew that I was being called to help people, to perhaps make an impact on a global level, but how? My life had a comfortable rhythm; I was married, had a stable career with a competitive salary, was in a graduate degree program for psychology, and had a wonderful circle of friends. What more did I need? I kept sensing that tugging but could not decipher what the "more" was. There were days when I felt like I was living someone else's life due to not fulfilling the mystery role I knew I was supposed to be living. I attempted to ignore that prompting, but I eventually gave in and sought out what it meant. I practiced Yoga, which led to meditation, which then progressed to learning about Buddhism. I began to express my deepest thoughts and emotions through journaling and delved into "self-help" books written by the likes of The Dalai Lama, Lama Surya Das, Sarah Ban Breathnach, Carolyn Myss and many others. My perception began to change and I clearly realized my situation: I recognized that fear was holding me back, learned that I am energetically connected to everyone on the planet, and acknowledged that my deeds and my emotional output affects everyone around me. I read that what I experienced is referred to as becoming "enlightened" and that I would never be able to view life in the same way again (which turned out to be a positive thing!).

I was on the fast track to learn as much as I could, hungry for as much spiritual knowledge and information as possible. I asked the Universe for guidance, and paths were created that connected me with the right people to assist me on my journey. I was directed to beneficial classes and workshops where I discovered tools that enabled me to soul search to my heart's content. Though I did not realize it at the time, I know now that it was divine guidance that led me every step of the way.

The next phase of ten years included a complete change of my life. I divorced, remarried, changed careers, and entered motherhood. At the beginning of that stage, I lost sight of the mission to discover my life's purpose and did not possess the desire to continue. I focused attention on enhancing my physical body by working out on a regular basis at the gym, going for long walks or runs, getting massages, and treating any health ailments with acupuncture and homeopathy. I left my stressful job, changed my diet to all natural and organic foods, and exchanged my toiletries for those that were devoid of toxins. I substituted cough drops for slippery elm lozenges, coffee for green tea, and used flower essences for stress. I became pregnant with my first child, a boy, in 2007, and began a difficult but fulfilling journey during the next decade.

Just sixteen months after my son came into this world, I gave birth to my daughter. Four months in with two babies, my son was diagnosed with Autism and life became too difficult and stressful for me to manage well. As mentally and physically exhausted as I was, I had to find a way to push on. The Autism diagnosis prompted me to research and seek out as many natural and alternative methods as possible to assist him with overcoming his challenges. We received assistance through an intensive early intervention program 12 hours per week which he began just a few months before he turned two. Early Intervention provided services to us until my son's third birthday, when he was then enrolled in preschool where he participated in skill-building groups and underwent Occupational Therapy and Applied Behavioral Analysis.

Two years after my son's Autism diagnosis, I was at my lowest point, my "rock bottom." I regretted making the choice to have children, and just like when I was 27 years old, I felt as though I was living the wrong life. I could not understand why God would allow an innocent child to become a victim of such a frustrating disability, and I began to doubt that a higher power even existed. Distraught and dispirited, I collected my self-help books and donated them to Goodwill. I was consumed by the difficulty of motherhood and the lack of energy to take care of my children, let alone myself. I desperately needed a break!

In an effort to relieve my depression in a holistic manner, I scoured the internet and found information about a specific company touting their essential oils as the best alternative option to medication. I was desperate for something natural that would help me feel more energetic, lose the baby weight, and manage my stress. I investigated the company's website and was appalled at how expensive the tiny bottles were, but read that these natural compounds had many health benefits that seemed too good to ignore. I proceeded to Amazon.com, found some from the company that was mentioned in the article for a significantly lower cost, and I purchased two bottle blends and one single oil bottle, along with a small fan diffuser.

A few years later at a craft fair, I noticed hordes of people gathered around a table of essential oils from a newer company that was competition to the one whose products I had previously purchased. I did not notice any benefits from the oils I had bought through Amazon, so I had zero interest to learn about this new company; in fact, I was repulsed. I could not understand why someone would pay so much money for these small bottles of liquid that I considered to be a fad, exaggerated hype, and of no benefit. It is obvious to me now that the Universe was attempting to guide me in the right direction, but I was not paying attention at all! A few months later, a friend of mine texted me and asked me what I thought about that newer brand of essential oils. I thought, "Oh no, not you, too!" but instead I replied that my opinion was that there was probably not much of a difference between brands; they were most likely all the same and they probably would not work for her the way they hadn't worked for me.

It is very quizzical to me now, years later, to look back and realize how wrong and close-minded I was. Perhaps it just wasn't the right time for me to venture on the path that would ultimately be the answer to that tugging I had felt so long ago. I can recognize now that I had a lot of inner turmoil that needed to be resolved first before I was equipped to help others.

Once both of my children were in school full-time and my schedule finally allowed time for me to engage in physical activity at the local gym, I discovered that I did not have the energy. I consulted with an Osteopathic doctor who gave me the discouraging diagnosis of adrenal fatigue, but I was thankful for a viable explanation of what I had been battling for several years. Since I was not interested in medication for my condition, I began to pay attention to my health for the first time in almost ten years. I found a balance between personal time and family time, rested extensively, and volunteered one to two times a week at my children's school. I began to have more energy and a positive outlook on motherhood, and on life in general. The following year, I felt ready to return to work which was a huge milestone after five years of exhaustion and stress! I was hired for a part-time position at a nearby high school where I worked with students who were expelled and suspended. In the following Fall, a new colleague joined me in the program. She confessed to me one day that she could see spirits of others' loved ones who had passed. She disclosed to me that I had a male spirit who was with me much of the time. I was very intrigued by this and began to feel spiritual belief re-emerge! I was determined to find out who this man was, though I intuitively knew that he was my paternal grandfather. I booked an appointment with a psychic medium who was referred to me by a friend. As soon as we began the session, she told me that I am an empath, meaning that I take on others' emotions as my own and that I need to learn how to protect myself from absorbing those energies. She confirmed my suspicions to be true about my grandfather being with me. He revealed to her that my zest for life reminded him of how he viewed his life, and that he loves to be around me because of the similarity. This brought tears to my eyes! How could I have doubted that the spiritual realm even existed? That session (though I had several more) revived my path to not only climb back on the wagon of seeking spirituality in my life, but this time I was on the expressway!

One experience led to another. I made a new friend at work who referred me to a Shaman, through whom I significantly learned about the connection that we humans have to the earth, and how that ties in spiritually. He taught me to visualize a ring of fire for protection and invited me to join a community circle. I was hungry for more, asking the Universe to lead me in the right direction to dynamic individuals who could assist me on this path of raising my vibration. I reconnected with an acquaintance from the past who referred me to a Shamanic practitioner who performed soul retrievals. That experience elevated my spirituality to a new level, lifting the 15 year burden of a writer's block in one fell swoop! This upgraded awakening that occurred in my life was the 2.0 version of what I had experienced twenty years earlier, and this time I knew that I had to fully embrace it and commit myself to the point of no return.

Around the same time that my upgraded spiritual journey was reborn, I learned of a neurological-based chiropractor, Dr. Ella, who uses a specific technique to measure the body under stress and how the brain responds to it. She is also able to determine how balanced or imbalanced the four quadrants of the brain are. I decided to have my son begin this treatment, as he also had a (mild) diagnosis of ADHD, and I was concerned about it progressing to the point where his Neurologist would prescribe medication. This type of chiropractic was extremely beneficial for him since Autism is explained as the brain being "wired" differently. Dr. Ella also suggested using essential oils. I was skeptical but agreed to try the adjustments first before adding in the oils. I gave it about a month and though my son experienced positive results with the chiropractic alone, Dr. Ella suggested that we give the essential oils a try. Once I began diffusing essential oils nightly in my son's room and applied essential oils topically to the back of his neck and bottoms of his feet, wow! I could not believe how much calmer he became and how his focus improved over the course of one year. I asked her why we were noticing such a huge difference with the oils (especially after I didn't have luck a few years prior), and she explained that it was most likely because the brand we were using now is "certified pure therapeutic grade" which is devoid of toxins and not diluted. I began using these natural concoctions for the rest of the family, including myself, and five years later, we still utilize them in our household for a multitude of uses. We diffuse lavender, vetiver, cedarwood, and sandalwood to aid with relaxation and sleep. We make homemade mosquito and tick repellent, foaming hand soap, and all-purpose kitchen cleaner. Using essential oils to nurture the body's natural healing abilities is truly a gift and replacing harsh and toxic chemicals is my dream come true! I found that I don't have to use much—"less is more"—therefore, I actually save money with these natural solutions!

Dr. Ella recommended a specific oil blend to help me feel grounded, which protects me from absorbing others' energies and emotions. She introduced me to a Yoga instructor who demonstrated how to use essential oils on chakra (energy) centers and who gave me a protocol for releasing emotional hooks. With applying these new practices over time, I slept better and noticed a huge difference with my metabolism. In addition, essential oils may enhance one's spiritual connection, inspire to seek out and fulfill life's destiny, assist with physically healing the body, and allow an individual to release unhealthy beliefs that are limiting.

The overall benefits and results that essential oils delivered to my family enthused me so much that I felt the calling to share with others! I was presented with the opportunity to enroll in an online certification program to become an essential oils coach. During this course, I was informed about the astounding benefits of the chemical constituents that are the lifeblood of plants, trees, and fruits. It was fascinating to me that frankincense and spikenard were used for their healing properties during Biblical times and that ancient peoples revered these plants as sacred gifts and spiritual tools.

I began teaching introductory and "DIY" classes through the Adult Education Department at the school where I worked. A year later, I created a wellness consultation and education business, and named it "Restoring Through Nature." Fortunately, I acquired a few enthusiastic clients right away who, after consulting with me, experienced positive results from using essential oils like my family has. Supporting and empowering others in this way confirmed to me that *this* was the first step to what the Universe intended for me to do so many years ago.

Have you ever taken a whiff of a scent and wondered why you may have associated it with something in particular? Besides an elicited memory, perhaps that aroma enabled you to feel happy or energetic. It is not necessary to have an association of a memory to alter or achieve a certain emotion; it is possible to create the desired outcome simply by matching an essential oil to the response you are attempting to achieve. For example, if you are in a relationship where you have the fear of rejection and are intimidated to expose your authentic self, inhaling lavender essential oil will send a message to your brain that it is safe to be open and to allow emotional honesty. In turn, allowing yourself to let go may encourage positive health throughout the body, as the power of scent is holistic and can affect the entire body in beneficial ways. This is due to the olfactory system being connected to the limbic system in the brain which controls sense of smell, and where emotions and memories are stored. Once a scent penetrates the nose, a response is created by the limbic system. Therefore, something pleasing such as the smell of cheesy pizza, your favorite scented candle, or an apple pie that your grandmother freshly baked will evoke a positive memory, thought, or emotion from which you originally associated the scent.

As a coach, I emphasize to my clients that an important part of being human is to feel emotions, whether they are joyful or painful. If someone experiences feelings of anger, hurt, sadness, or other disconcerting emotions, essential oils may offer assistance as he or she strives to completely release these emotions from within. It is of utmost importance that we allow our emotions to flow if we long to be healed from past hurt or negative encounters. Sometimes, pain can block the flow and can render an individual "stuck" and unable to truly feel a certain emotion. As daunting as it may sound to potentially conjure up past, stuck emotions, the reward is liberation from the binding chains once and for all.

Currently, I meet with clients virtually to conduct wellness consultations and to suggest essential oils that may ease their various health concerns. My goal is to guide each client to become his or her own B.O.S.S.: **balanced** in health; **open** to learning new ways to reach optimum health; **sensible** in choosing what is put on and in the body to enhance physical, emotional, and spiritual wellbeing; and **strong** in the knowledge of what is personally best. Gaining control of one's health requires the desire and courage to implement a change. That may challenge someone to perhaps venture "outside the box" from his or her comfort zone, but the relief that essential oils may deliver to individuals truly goes beyond what is in the bottle!

The earth lavishes us with everything that we need to heal, flourish, and learn about ourselves to promote growth. The vital force that lies within essential oils is a sacred gift given to humanity from our earth mother, through which every individual can support his or her mind, body and spirit to fulfill his or her life's purpose.

ABOUT THE AUTHOR

ELISSA NAUMAN

Elissa "Elle" Nauman is a health educator, coach and the owner of Restoring Through Nature, LLC. She guides clients to achieve their physical, emotional and spiritual health goals through the support of essential oils. She has a Master of Science in Counseling and Psychological Services, is a Certified Essential Oils Coach, and is currently enrolled in a Chakra Therapist Certification program.

Elle began her journey almost 30 years ago of discovering first-hand how to incorporate health into every aspect of her life. She uses a proprietary method with her clients, teaching them to take control of their health through knowledge and personal empowerment.

Elle resides in Maine where she teaches introductory essential oil classes and "DIY" workshops in addition to her coaching business. She enjoys nature walks, creating plant-based recipes, and painting and crafting with her children.

Business name: Restoring Through Nature, LLC

Website: restoringthroughnature.com
Email: elissa@restoringthroughnature.com
Facebook: https://www.facebook.com/restoringthroughnature

KALAIN HILDERBRAND

SEER OF THE NEW EARTH

*W*hen I was a young child, I remember playing with Angels! They would always play with me and leave me feathers, and I would always put them up in a bible. I remember when something didn't go right, I would close my eyes and shake. Like I just knew in my soul I was this magical being! I remember the Angels saying I'm meant for great things in this life, that I'm here with a crowd of great ones, called the "Golden Children, Golden Ray, Children of the Sun" with a golden aura or shine.

I was outside all the time as much as possible! I was a child who didn't mind being alone and playing with animals, critters, climbing, and hugging trees, looking at the clouds and their shapes like they were signs, a star gazer, making mud pies, and always had to add little plants and flowers (which I now know by the smell, were herbs and medicine). Everywhere I went, I collected rocks (now I know they were crystals) and I even saw ghosts!

It all pretty much stopped when I started school, however. I soon got lost in the brainwashing of how I should be, act, think, etc., until I completely lost myself. I still always played outside, but I became more introverted, a rebel against systems. I started feeling angry and lost because I felt so very different from everyone around me. I started getting in trouble at school and running away from home to live outside. I didn't feel at home anywhere, but outside with nobody around. I started getting depressed and tried suicide a few times and was put in a hospital ward for mentally ill people. They put me on so much medication for so many years. It got way worse for me. It felt like I was spiraling out of control, and I missed what I had as a young child! I was so angry at the Angels for leaving me!! I felt so alone!

When I was around 12-13 years old, I woke up to a UFO flying off right outside my window. I then started wearing alien shirts and remember people saying I was so weird! So, needless to say, I started believing maybe I was!

There were others who embraced me and loved my "weirdness, however. A lot of people, including adults, would seek me out for advice and say I made them feel so much better, healed, a breath of fresh air. Like they could trust me and feel protected. Some were drawn to me like a magnet, while others didn't even seem to be aware of my presence.

When I look back, I see I was a very protected individual!

My dad came home from work one day, and he took a shower to get ready for family counseling. When he got out of the shower, he saw that the new Camaro he had just driven home from work in had a flat tire. I mean, all the way flat in less than a half-hour, so we had to take the older truck. We were on Highway 44, and a semi went to get over and didn't see the other car. That car then went sideways right in front of us, and my dad swerved and hit the guardrail going 70 mph! Had I been in that Camaro, we wouldn't be here or writing this story! So, we didn't make it to counseling. However, we landed in the hospital with minor cuts and bruises. None of us had on a seatbelt, and my face broke the windshield. When we went back later to see the truck damages at the junkyard, we found my blood and hair in the shattered windshield, yet all I had was a swollen knot under my eye and a black eye!

The more I've learned to follow my heart and guidance, the more gifts come to me. Over time, since childhood, and overcoming my differences with others and still loving myself and believing in myself, I have mastered clairaudience, meaning I hear spirits in my head, clairvoyance, meaning I see things in my head, claircognizant, a nagging "knowing", and clairsentient, meaning I just feel my way intuitively around in all areas of my life. I'm also a master manifestor, I can manipulate the weather, as well as feel when a storm is coming from very far away. I'm highly sensitive to any energy! I can pick up on lies and how people are feeling; I'm a high empath.

I realize now that some people couldn't handle me or see me because I was a much higher, in tuned, vibration than most. How did I get to that level? Better yet, how can YOU reach that level?! Well, loving yourself and believing in yourself and the higher realms with unwavering faith opens you up more to receive from them.

Be excited when you see them help you, for example when they leave you a message like number patterns (11:11, 4:44, 12:34), etc., or any repeating number pattern continually coming to your awareness through a clock, receipt total, license plates, billboards, etc. Then look it up! Once you start trusting they're there, seeing the signs, looking up the signs, following the signs, you're opening yourself up to them and trusting.

I received so many feathers as a child, and now again. I always look up the bird meaning, the color of the feather meaning then take the advice and always thank them. I never let money, status, systems, fame, or any earthly thing get in the way of what they say. Which has formed a beautiful bond between spirit and I after my awakening in 2011.

In the Bible, it says, "Be in this world, but not of it," as well as, "Be as a child," "Knock and the door shall be opened," "seek and ye shall find," "the truth shall set you free." Those are my mottos! If you listen to yourself, no matter how crazy it may seem, follow the signs and your heart and soul, you can't lose in spirit. Yes, it could be challenging if you're holding on to what people may think, but ultimately we can't change the Earth or go to the New Earth with old, limiting beliefs that are outdated.

We have to BE the change, embody the change, want the change, and absolutely let nobody stop us, right?! If you're looking for your gifts and who you are... that's ultimately the best place to start. Especially if you deal with confidence issues because you always listened to people or society say you're wrong, delusional, weird, etc. The best place to start is within what your desires are, no matter how big or small, using and practicing your clairs because we all have them—knowing that there's no such thing as coincidence. The more you search there, the more signs you receive to the next steps.

I started researching my numerology chart, my astrological chart, my human design chart, my personality tests. So what I found out about myself through these avenues is I'm meant to be a spiritual leader (life path 1, destiny 7). My husband and I are twin flames and meant to change the world. I'm a manifestor and mystical, I'm meant to write a book, I'm the black sheep of the family, people are drawn to my honesty and knowledge because I hold so much of it and don't hold back out of fear. Anything I could go back all the way to childhood and relate to of why exactly I was so different! It opened so many doors for me, as well, and I really started loving myself and my uniqueness.

Now people come to me for just about everything and say they felt led, called, pulled, guided. They come to me for herbal remedies or for bible advice (I'm an ordained minister, but please don't put me in that box, I see the Bible way differently, and I'm not like any you've met). They come to me for healing or to ask questions on what they should do about a problem they're facing. They come to me for my readings and intuition. Some just find me fascinating and want to get to know more about me. I just know the more I stayed in my lane and listened to myself and the guidance of my angels and guides didn't let people push me around any longer in what I should think and believe, the more and more doors opened and people flocked my way.

A pure heart and love for all beings is the highest vibration. Having the whole world's interests at heart, as well as the plants, animals, trees, bugs. We all play a part in our roles and are all very important. Watching television, listening to loud, angry music, and listening to others when it didn't feel right had to go. I learned to stay away from the toxicity and beehive mind it brought me that really depressed me before. It has a way of clouding your judgment and inner knowing. I started listening to high-frequency music instead and working on myself and my inner world. Asking the questions, who am I? What do I believe in? What can I do to make this world a brighter place for all? What do I need to change in myself and my subconscious to bring these changes? Sometimes, all you really need to do is look back to your early childhood, when your imagination was active, and work your way up to heal, transmute, and learn from all you've been through. We can't possibly know what we want until we clearly know what we don't want.

When you start to look outside the box of what you've been taught, and start seeking the bigger questions in life and turn inward, you eventually come to the realization that God's name really is, I AM, that we really were made in source image. That you really did have the power within all along, like, Dorothy, in The Wizard Of Oz!

When you reach that point of power, knowing you've been around for many lifetimes, and remember, then your fear of "death" goes away, your fear of someone doing you wrong goes away. You start manifesting the things you do want and wish to see for the whole world because we can't be happy truly unless everyone is.

You start to tap into your healing capabilities, your clairs and intuition, you start talking and co-creating with spirit and your higher-self, wanting more and more. If you want to start communicating with spirit through means of divination or metaphysical tools or even just asking for signs and synchronicities, I always suggest you raise your frequency and ground by hugging trees, picking up trash off Mother Earth, walk barefoot, and trust first. You do attract your vibrational match always! A low vibration attracts low vibration things. That's what narcissism and schizophrenia are. I always raise my frequency with meditation, high-frequency music, nature, truth, love for all. I have found that YouTube is getting really good with having a wide variety of modalities in music and meditation, as well as hypnosis, mantras, shamanic music. I loved researching the mudras and mantras together; those are powerful as well. It's really all about the intentions behind what you're looking for that makes the difference.

I love to pick cards by their gentleness and positivity. The ones I feel drawn to. If I don't like a tarot card or a rune, I simply won't use them. If we create our reality, why would I want anything negative? I make my own crystal jewelry and pendulums as well because I feel better knowing my energy and light is in them, and I don't feel I'm giving my power away, yet I'm truly trusting my guides, Angels, and Higher-self. The same is true for books, crystals, and classes that I take. I just feel the energy and have a clear "knowing" if I want them or not. If the name lights me up, the energy of it, or any good "feeling" that's when I know It's right for me. I never went by who was the most popular spiritual teacher or bestseller.

You know It's your Angels guiding you, or your higher-self, when something lights you up. When you are so passionate about helping yourself and the whole, as one. At this point in time, pretty much everyone is feeling the pull or calling. A knowing that there's so much more and this isn't the end, but a new beginning. People are coming together and bringing peace and love to one another. This pandemic has really opened many minds and hearts! We are at a fork in the road — do we want what we had, or do we really want a new way of being and truly connecting and putting our differences and divisions aside. It's ultimately up to us to co-create this, but we do have free will to relive the wars and divisions. Some people will stay in a 3D reality if they so choose, and that's fine. They signed up and wanted to learn more or need to. Others will go to 4D and 5D because they have learned, and none of these lessons suit them any longer. They are ready to master their spirit because they've already mastered the Karma and material world. We will be back in our crystalline bodies because of our high vibration, like the Angels.

I know to some, this seems far-fetched or like you're not going to make it. Shadow work is really hard! I do, however, promise that if you feel what I'm writing, you will make it! It does take time, which is why this is such a long window of opportunity astrology-wise. It feels like ten steps forward, 100 steps back, over and over. Just like all your life, thus far, has been. If you look back on your life, you'll see you were always growing at all times. You see the bad differently than you did while it was happening. You come to a point where you say, well, if that didn't happen, I wouldn't be who and what I am today. You can then start to see what led to different blocks and challenges in your life and how to better go around them next time to change that repetition. Once a lesson is learned or a fear is overcome, you never have to repeat it. It's done! Take a challenge today that would normally upset you or make you angry, and instead, take a deep breath and send it love and forgiveness. Do something opposite of how you would normally have done it. Watch how your world starts to change before your very eyes. It really is that easy and magical.

Once you start doing that consciously every day, it will become a habit in your subconscious. You will manifest and create a new reality just by intentionally changing your habits and reactions. You have complete power over your feelings and reactions and the Karma you create.

I would like to suggest looking into the 12 Universal Laws.
1.) The Law of Divine Oneness, we are all one, created by the same creator.

2.) The Law Of Vibration, everything is energy. You attract your vibrational frequency.

3.) The Law Of Action, faith, and trust is step one. Action is always the step that gets you there. It's your added intention behind your actions that bring your manifestation.

4.) Law Of Cause And Effect, every action and thought has an equal and opposite reaction.

5.) Law Of Compensation, AKA Karma, what goes around, comes around. What you put out into the Universe always comes back.

6.) The Law Of Correspondence, as above so below, as within, so without.

7.) The Law Of Attraction, aligning your thoughts with your wishes and desires. Being a vibrational match for what you seek.

8.) The Law Of Perpetual Transmutation, being the change we wish to see for the betterment of ourselves and the world around us.

9.) The Law Of Relativity, being grateful for everything, even challenges. Knowing that things could always be worse, and someone out there has it worse right now.

10.) The Law Of Polarity, everything on Earth has an opposite.

11.) The Law Of Rhythm, everything has a perfect timing and natural rhythm. Last but not least,

12.) The Law Of Gender, feminine and masculine energy resides in everything on this Earth. The secret is to balance it.

In astrology, things are ripe for a new Earth and to do things completely differently. It started in 2012 and ends in 2040. It's a small window to do the work and seek something different and more loving and freeing. I see a lot of current systems failing, better technology like, super fruits and vegetables that have all nutrients to survive will emerge. We will be able to tap more into our natural talents and abilities we were born with, rather than school like it is now. The people who abuse their powers will fall to the bottom, and the ones using it for the betterment of the all will rise to the top. We will have better travel, with no pollution. More solar power and free energy. Natural products and no more pharmaceuticals that are harmful. We will be more conscious of our surroundings and what we feed our temples (bodies, minds, and spirits). We will have our DNA upgraded to our original blueprint, meaning our gifts of healing, telepathic abilities, and hearts will be fully open and functional. We will have crystal healing domes and houses and high-frequency music or vibrations because we all will be raised to those frequencies. We will eventually be so powerful, our gifts of telekinesis will come back, and we can astral travel, build and tear down our creations and homes, etc. It truly is an exciting time, so remember, it's all in the journey and not the destination. We are, and always have been, infinite beings.

ABOUT THE AUTHOR

KALAIN HILDERBRAND

Kalain Hilderbrand is an Ordained Minister who blesses all she comes into contact with, as well as their homes. She is a Reiki Master, who incorporates her Shamanic and natural abilities to her healing modalities. She has been reading Oracle cards, Pendulums, Tea leaves, and runes for the last 6 years. She is a spiritual mentor to many and has many great reviews everywhere she goes.

She's been self taught in most areas including studying, herbal, homeopathic remedies, pressure point therapy, massage therapy, auric field energy clearing, numerology, and astrology for the last 10 years or so. She is also a Lumerian High Preistess, Crystal Healer, and works with Angels and auras and is a meditation teacher. She is a wayshower, bridges Heaven and Earth, a Gatekeeper, Earth Angel.

She is a proud wife to her amazing husband, Thomas, and a mother to 3 amazing, gifted young adults, Koby, Khayle, and Kaydence. They live in Illinois and love the nature time as much as they can. If you see her hugging a tree, planting something, or cleaning up trash off our beautiful, Earth Mother, please feel free to come join her!!!

Divine I AM website: https://linktr.ee/TheDivineIAM?
YouTube: The Divine I Am
Facebook: https://www.facebook.com/groups/TheDivineIAM/?ref=share
Email: Kohilderbrand32@gmail.com
Facebook: https://www.facebook.com/kalain.ormsby
Would like to donate: paypal.me/kohilderbrand

DESIREE BARTON

EVERYTHING ON OUR PATH HAS A PURPOSE

My name is Desiree, most people call me Desi. I'm so honored to be writing these words of encouragement, truth, experience, and accession. I live in sunny Arizona, where I own a beautiful home with my husband. I'm a bonus mom to 3 wonderful children and a proud dog mom. I have chosen not to have any children of my own. I have ventured off to become a Life Coach due to previous events that took place in my life.

It did not always look like this, though. I grew up in what some would call a dysfunctional household. My parents did their best with what they had, but love wasn't between them. There was a lot of fighting over the years. It was not a good example of what a loving relationship should look like. However, we had a roof over our heads, played sports, and most of the time food in our belly.

As the years went on, my mom would always say how one day, she would get a job so she could leave my dad. At the time, she was a stay-at-home mom raising four children while my dad worked a blue-collar job in construction to provide for us.

Eventually, my mom was able to get her Real Estate license. This gave her the flexibility to take care of the kids and work. Over time the demands of work along with being a parent grew heavier. A lot of responsibility became mine. As some parents do, they turn to alternatives to help keep up with the demands of life. My mother's choice was meth. Meth makes you feel on top of the world, and it gives you so much energy that you feel you can accomplish anything with confidence.

When these changes started to occur, I was in high school. My mother did not come home until early mornings. I used to stay up worrying about her for hours, looking out the front door window. Dad left early in the morning to go to work. My younger siblings needed to eat and get to school, so I stepped up to the plate to help them continue to live a normal life.

This put a lot of pressure on me. I felt hurt. I felt so lost, broken, and negated, I didn't know how to deal with the emotional pain going throughout my body.

Fifteen was the last normal year as a child I could remember. I had already been a wild child going to parties, drinking, and experimenting with drugs. I was still trying to hide it from my parents at that age.

It was around that time my life started to change. The emotions got heavier to handle, and not knowing how to process them, I turned to meth. I thought to myself, "well, my mom is doing it, so why shouldn't I?" I decided to take it from her the first time I wanted to try it, and I was immediately hooked! I felt like I was untouchable on cloud 9. It was the most euphoric feeling I had ever come across, and even better is I did not feel my emotions anymore! This was the first time I knowingly numbed my emotions. It took me hard and fast, seemingly answering all my problems.

Eventually, my mom got an apartment, and we moved out to the house I spent the majority of my life in. Not knowing that I was so attached to this place I called home it pushed me deeper into my addiction because that pain hit even harder, the pain I didn't know how to deal with.

We are not taught in school how to deal with anger, betrayal, sadness, hurt, loss, or any of the array of emotions we feel during our time here on earth. We continue to go through life being the same young child who got hurt, making us play out the same situations over again in our life. Only this time we have built walls that try to keep us safe but only end up hurting us more. We chose to act in a certain way to protect ourselves. Or we keep letting the same patterns play out in our lives because we never did the healing work.

I started to hang out with people that were addicted to drugs, and with that came dating those people. The first abuse I encountered was around 16 years old. My little sister was at the apartment we just moved into with one of their friends. They heard the ruckus in the room and came running in to find my boyfriend at the time choking me.

This would be a pattern that continued to play out in my life over the years.

As my mom moved us into the apartment, she was also in her own abusive love addiction and on drugs. The situation just got worse. It was a spiral further into our addictions. We tried our hardest to do what was right but also numbed our emotions with drugs.

One weekend my mom finally had enough of my drug use and told me I was going to live with family up north so I could get sober. By the grace of God, this was the best thing that could have happened for my life at that time. I had already missed around 60 days of my senior year. My uncle, who at the time was a principal, called my school to get all of the work I had missed to make up while I stayed. Right when I got to San Luis Obispo, CA, my aunt got suddenly very sick. While I stayed there to get my schoolwork done, I was able to help take care of my aunt because the doctors couldn't figure out what was wrong. Many doctors' appointments and sick days later, my aunt was diagnosed with a brain tumor in which she survived.

God, Angels, Universe had this planned out in a way we could have never imagined to help each other.

I ended up barely graduating high school. I felt so grateful and happy that I was able to graduate with my class. Unfortunately, as most addicts do, I relapsed. Things were still tough at home. My dad was trying to find out where we lived to do his best for us kids, but my mom hid it from him. It was truly madness.

My addiction got worse. I ended up hanging out with much older drug addicts and went further down the rabbit hole of addiction. At different points, I had a shotgun held to my head, I stole a car and drove it off a cliff to not get caught, started selling drugs, and the last straw was the checks I stole to get my next fix. See, when you are addicted to drugs, you don't care about anyone or anything other than getting high and not coming down. Nothing else is important!!

This led to the day I got arrested. It was a familiar kind of morning where I was trying to figure out how I was going to get my next high. As I hung out in a hotel room with other addicts trying to figure out how to get money, I told them that I had blank checks that I stole.

One of the girls told me how she just opened up a bank account to cash a fake check and didn't get caught.

The next day, we went into the bank, and she acted as my aunt. Being that I was 17 and it's graduation season, we wrote a check out to me as it was a gift for graduating.

As we tried to open the account, I could tell the staff knew something was off, but my addiction roared louder in my ear than anything else that I could hear.

I sat there wearing a tiny yellow top with a short cut-off jean skirt and a tiny knife in my skirt as I never knew when I would need protection from the life I was living.

As I looked at the doors, I saw the officer come through. I immediately knew it was for us. The thought of running went through my mind, but I tried that previously when I got caught shoplifting, in which I did not get very far.

The rest was a blur other than being told that I had to go to Juvenile Hall due to my prior record. As they sat me up late at night to take me to Downey, CA, I said, "don't I get a phone call?" Reluctantly they gave me a call. Once again, by the grace of God, my mother answered the phone. At this time, we had moved back to my childhood home, and It was a very slim chance that anyone would answer, being that cell phones were not around. As I told my mom what happened, I could hear the tears in her voice saying, "Be Strong, don't show them you are scared. We will get you out."

I got arrested on a Wednesday, and it happened to be a holiday weekend which meant I spent five days there before I could see a judge. I was coming down from drugs and needed to sleep with very little function after being up for so many days. It was terrifying not having any idea what to expect.

I was in so much emotional pain sitting in juvenile hall that I knew one day I was going to turn my life around to help others because no one should ever have to feel the type of pain I felt over the years with no one to turn to.

Being in there was exactly the moment of clarity that my young mind needed. I saw the light at the end of the tunnel and knew, sitting on that dayroom floor coming down off of drugs, that I did not want to live a life like that any longer. I remember the clear voice in my head. I can still hear it today 18 years later "if you keep living this life, you will be dead or in prison the rest of your life by 21". My soul roared loudly and said, "This is not what you came here to do or who you are meant to be."

God knew exactly what I needed to get my life back on track. I finally got to go to court, which seemed like an eternity. My family was there to support me.

I sat with the public defender looking over my charges. She told me, "You have six felonies and have already been in trouble prior to this arrest. You will be lucky not to be tried as an adult. These are federal crimes, and chances are you will get a few years." The sickening gut feeling I felt that day was something I never experienced before. This all made me grow up even faster.

I thought my life was truly over, and it would have been if it wasn't for my mom!

Even though she was in her own addiction, she went to work to find a rehab for me to go to. Through my dad's insurance, she found a place in Orange County, California.

The public defender told the judge that my parents had found a rehabilitation center for minors under 18 and thought that it would be a better alternative than prison.

After some thought, the judge told me, "If you come back and complete the 30 days with no issues, I will expunge your record."

"What, are you kidding me? Am I actually hearing this correctly?" I can't believe what I'm hearing from the judge.

"This was my chance," I thought to myself.

I should have been processed in federal court. This was the saving grace I was praying for. I was able to leave that day with my Grandma, Dad, Brother, Mom, and Sister-in-Law. The feeling I experienced was almost unexplainable! I was petrified for what was ahead, but I was also relieved that I had a second chance!

I spent the next 30 days working on myself. It was very difficult to look in the mirror, and at the decisions I made. I didn't care about myself, and now I was coming into a place where I had to own my actions.

I was astonished that there was a place for alcoholics and addicts to get sober together. I had no idea about AA or NA meetings before I went to rehab. I finally did not feel so alone!

I started to mend the relationship with myself, which was not an easy task. I hated who I was. I could not pull the lies I normally would with these counselors. After my mom had left from a family visit, they asked me if she did drugs, still being naive, I tried to protect her and told them no, but they knew the truth.

During family therapy, they had me confront my mom in the middle of the family group. It was terrifying. I remember the look she gave me as she said, "how dare you," and got up and left. My dad followed. That would have left me alone to process the next few weeks, but my brother and his wife were there for me. If they had not been there, I would have left rehab. There were many times I thought about leaving even with the serious charges against me.

If you never dealt with addiction before, you probably think, how could I ever think about leaving, which would absolutely ruin my life. Addiction takes over all logical thinking. It consumes every part of your soul and being. It destroys anything in its way!

With the odds against me, I succeeded and completed the 30 days of rehab. It was such a glorious feeling! I went back before that judge so proud! Even though I was still on probation and had to drug test eventually with a clean history, the judge followed through and sealed my juvenile record!

I felt so truly blessed for the chance I was given!

After rehab, I went to a sober living with twelve other women, and I shared a big room with six others. This was the first adult decision I made for the better in my life. I knew if I went back home, I would have ended up relapsing.

My dad helped for the first few months, but eventually, I had to make the decision to move back home or stay. I knew if I went back home, I would have relapsed. I wasn't strong enough yet. I worked three jobs at one point to afford my stay to make sure I didn't have to go back home.

Then the unthinkable happened. My mom, still addicted, ended up getting in trouble. At this point, everyone had disowned her. I was the only one that understood the grips of addiction and would go visit her.

I remember the day she told me she got sentenced. Through the glass with the phones to our ears, she told me that they gave her five years which she would have to complete 85% of that time. I was devastated. I remember walking out of the jail bawling and people asking if I was ok.

I was young and still needed my mom, the mom who was my best friend growing up. Even though that seemed like a harsh sentence at the time, God knew exactly what it would take for her to turn her life around. Ever since the day my mom got out, she has led a clean life!

I eventually moved out of the sober living to get an apartment and stayed in Orange Country for ten years.

I got my first office job as a receptionist and worked my way up from there over the years.

My life seemed normal but not doing the deep healing work from the past continued to play out in my life. I dated the wrong guys. I was angry. I was insecure. I was jealous. I yelled a lot. I didn't trust anyone. This led me on a road of attracting the wrong people. Or if it was a good person, I would ruin it in some way because I never felt worthy of anything good.

This eventually led to a five-year abusive relationship which diminished me in ways no one should have to go through!

He had open wounds of trauma that were never addressed. We both did, so we attracted each other.

It fed into the past emotional hurt I had not dealt with. The name-calling was familiar as I heard it growing up in my parent's relationship.

When we do not take time to do the deeper healing work of our past, the trauma continues to play out in our lives.

Even though I wasn't addicted to drugs anymore, I replaced it with other destructive behaviors and didn't even know it.

I never learned how to deal with those painful emotions from when I was a kid. Every time we would break up, it felt like I was going to die. Ever feel like that before? The pain is so unbearable you can barely catch your breath from crying, it feels like the world is going to stop, and you don't know what to do with yourself? This was from years of un-processed trauma.

In order to stop the excruciating pain that took over my body, I would go back even though I knew it was wrong, even though every ounce of me wanted out. I was hell-bent that I was going to make this relationship work!

I didn't know at the time that I was trying to fix this relationship because it reminded me of my parents. This time it was going to be different, and I would prove my self-centered ego right!

Eventually, that ended, and I began to look inward. Why did I keep dating the same people? Why did I keep making destructive decisions? How come I was never really happy?

For the first time in a while, I walked into church and leaned on God to help get back some self-worth. I prayed every day for healing and eventually to bring the right person into my life.

I met my husband, and as our relationship grew, we discovered that we had been praying for each other. Jason and I have had to work through our own wounds, and I am so grateful we are both willing to keep loving each other.

After we got married, I was given the blessing of re-thinking my line of work. I was miserable at my corporate job.

As I sat thinking about what path I wanted to take, the memory of the cold day in Juvenile Hall flashed in my mind. "How could you help others heal from their past pain so they can start to live a truly happy life?"

That is when my life really began to ascend to a place I did not know possible. I invested in a high-end coaching program in which I had to do my own healing work before helping others. I get to lead other souls through what I have already experienced and applied for myself.

There have been a lot of great tools that I have learned, lots of healing work that I get to take my client through. It truly lights me up working with others to heal from the past!

There have been two pivotal tools that have shifted my life and gave me freedom that I would like to share with you. The first one I would like to share is forgiveness and no, not forgiveness to anyone else but to yourself!

I would wake up in the morning, heart pounding with anxiety from nightmares of addiction and abuse that were still occurring many years later. I tried different things to help the guilt of my past, the shame that crept in my body, the judgment of my actions to go away. It wasn't until I truly forgave myself that I became free of the shackles of the past.

The truth is we deserve forgiveness more than anyone. We all have been dealt different hands throughout our lives, trying to do our best and sometimes making very poor decisions.

Forgiveness is the key to freedom. When we forgive ourselves, we start to heal the wounds of our past, so they no longer have room to play out in our current life.

The destructive behaviors start to dismantle.

The other is connecting to my inner child. It was not the five year old girl I thought needed healing but my teenage self. I was still a child when I was forced to grow up when I decided to numb my emotions above all else rather than take care of myself.

I needed to meet that younger part of myself as an evolved woman and apologize for the actions I took. I reassured my inner child that I was there for her now, and I would not abandon her again.

Connecting to your inner child does not mean reliving the tough times. You do not have to go back in time and feel those emotions all over again. Our inner child is still within us, and when we connect to that part of ourselves, the little girl that throws fits, gets jealous, and acts out, starts to feel loved.

These two amazing tools are the tip of the iceberg to start healing so you can live a life that makes you feel happy, fulfilled, understood, and accepted.

ABOUT THE AUTHOR

DESIREE BARTON

Desiree Barton is the Founder and CEO of Fierce Soul Living.
From the age of 17, she knew she wanted to help others when she
found herself addicted to drugs. Desiree now helps women turn
their past emotional pain into their power so they can feel confident,
leaving behind anxiety and worry to truly live the life they desire!

Using her intuition and breathwork she coaches her clients and
guides them to reach their fullest healing. Desiree lives in sunny
Arizona with her husband, dogs, and family where she loves to bask
in the sun, making memories that last a lifetime.

Website: www.fiercesoulliving.com
Email: desi.barton1@gmail.com
FB Group: Build Confidence with Self Care:Making Changes
Through Community
https://www.facebook.com/groups/339778967440213
Instagram https://www.instagram.com/desi_barton/

HANNAH WATSON

MY DARKEST DEPTHS TURNED INTO MY GREATEST STRENGTH

My emotions used to hurt so much that I shut myself off from them.

Not intentionally, you have to understand. From the outside I've always looked like I had it all together; I was a book-worm and an only child. I read my way through the entirety of the reading tree in my first year at school, learning came so easily to me. And I certainly didn't seem to need much in the way of anything, I was so self-sufficient, so self-assured and so accomplished.

The teacher's pet, straight A student, oldest (and therefore most responsible) one in the year—that version of me held together pretty well for the first few years of my schooling. But when I look back, there are hints of the running away I was doing; escapism into fictional worlds for one. Not that being a bookworm is a bad thing– far from it! And yet even before I had started school, I had already developed one of my main coping strategies: feeling fictional emotions, so I didn't have to feel my own.

The first signs of my repressed emotions showed up as cracks, in my perfectly constructed shell. Any bit of loose skin, old scabs, spots were a fair target, picked at until they bled, scabbed over and the physical cycle continued. From the outside it looked like "a bad habit." On the inside, this was my younger self's best way of trying to deal with emotional turmoil and being highly physically sensitive, but without the insight to describe what was going on and the knowledge to do anything about it.

My shame at being unable to stop myself was strong. I felt it physically, as hot flushes through my body and mentally, as a chorus of spiteful monkeys chattering away in my head, saying things like —"You should be able to stop this. Why can't you stop it? See— you're no good, you can't even do this simple thing" and the heart-squeezing pain that would clench my chest, making me feel small, cold and bad. I wish I had had some of the many tools I do now, to ride these strong emotional waves, such as this simple self-soothing practice.

Self-soothing for strong emotions practice:

Visualise a ball of green light at your heart, spinning wildly on its axis, switching erratically in the direction that it is spinning. As you place your dominant hand on your heart (or stroke your thumb on your index finger, if you need a more subtle gesture) and slow your breathing, see the green ball start to slow and rotate in one direction.

Stepping into the green ball, see the most innocent version of yourself, as a hurt, crying baby. Scope her up in your adult arms, rocking her, soothing her and telling her that you are here for her.

Note—if the emotional wave has deeper hurts attached to it, this practice will not fully dissipate the emotion, but should help take the edge off the depth of feeling, for you to then be able to use other tools and techniques to alleviate the emotion.

Feeling small was exacerbated by being bullied throughout the majority of my school life, knocking my confidence. Things that were once a source of pride, such as doing so well at school, became something I was targeted for, so I quickly learned that it was best to keep my head down and not be proud of what I had achieved.

GCSE revision week (age 16) was another major crack in my "perfect" shell. All the pressure, all my thoughts about not being able to cope, and the feeling of wanting to crawl out of my own skin, coupled with being left on my own at home while Mum was at work, turned out to be the perfect storm in a teacup for my depression to sidle through a crack and start wreaking havoc with my life. Unused to feeling unable to cope, I'd secretly watch Buffy videos until Mum came home from work and make it look like I had been revising my exam preparation notes all day. The weight in my chest, the heaviness on my shoulders and the black in my heart, with the nefarious whispers of "I can't do this. I can't cope" would drive me to seek distraction every single time.

Passing my GCSE exams with the highest grades, meant I got away with these distractions as a temporary plaster on the wound of my depression. My anxiety was not helped by further bullying in my final school years, including one guy in particular, who gifted me the lovely moniker "Gremlin," which of course stuck for years in my head as my beating myself up nickname of choice!

My time at University saw me putting more plasters on the wounds of my anxiety and my depression. I was living alone for the first time (albeit in halls), away from family and my long-term boyfriend. My final year I skipped most of my lectures, barely made it into my work-practice placement 3 days a week, and the habit I'd built of staying up late to finish off essays, turned into full on all-nighters the day before hand-in, fuelled by Coca-Cola and sausage rolls (to try and lessen the stomach churning effects of all those bubbles!). And yet even with final deadlines looming, I'd still find myself reading fanfiction, or watching a TV series of choice, as the yawning black depths of fear, the feeling of bubbles racing in my blood vessels and the skin prickling proved too much for me to handle and I would seek something, anything to distract me from those feelings.

And again, I felt like I couldn't tell anyone. Not my boyfriend. Not my parents. I hadn't really made any friends at University and I'd gotten pretty handy with believable stories about not having attended lectures, so to the outside world, I still looked like I had it all together.

But inside I was a roiling mess. The shell I had unconsciously created at such a young age, against feeling my own feelings, couldn't stand up under the weight of these emotions and continued to crack, and crack, and crack. Until one day there weren't enough plasters to hold it together anymore and it finally shattered in a doctor's office in London. Going in for antibiotics for a urinary tract infection and coming out with a tentative diagnosis of Seasonal Affective Disorder (seasonal depression) was the beginning of the race to the bottom of my black hole, whilst simultaneously starting to climb out of it, too.

By this point, my emotions had been running havoc for a good 15 years or so. And it would take another near decade of various attempts at psychological therapies, to start to level that playing field. Having a practice, such as this one, would have made that feeling of hitting rock bottom much, much more manageable.

Building back from shattered practice:

Visualise a cracked egg shell that has fallen all around you; a visual metaphor of your feelings, perhaps your life, right now. It can seem as though the pieces will never go back together, but the Japanese have the art of Kintsugi, where broken things are repaired with golden glue – showing the strength and the uniqueness in the rebuilding.

See the shattered pieces rise up around you, now with spaces in between, reforming that egg shape as best they can. The egg shape is larger than it was before, as you begin to paint the golden glue in between the floating pieces. See and feel the shattered pieces bonding back together around you - strengthened by the golden glue. You are now more expansive, stronger and more unique for what you have experienced.

You can repeat this energetics practice, reinforcing the bonds of the golden glue and so reinforcing your new expansion and growth, as much as you need to.

The roller coaster of those 25 years, of not knowing what I was experiencing, how to handle it—or that I could feel any different, are not an experience I would wish on my worst enemy. The pressure. The fear. The shame. The "not knowing if I can do this." The intense self-loathing. These are things I hope you never feel and yet I know all too well that so many of us do.

It had always been easier to do, to have my successes noticed and praised, than it was to be ok in my own company. And whilst being an overly-organised Virgo and driven spirit can have its advantages for achieving things, at the end of the day, that had been at the cost of my comfort in my own skin, my ability to connect truly with others, and a constant sense of not being good enough (no matter what I did).

I am passion and pleasure. Fire and starlight.
I am Human and Divine.
Multitudes are contained within me.

When you can walk into a concentration camp and feel the pain and suffering in the air, the blackness of the death, the blueness of the sorrow and the tingle down your spine at the horror the very earth has witnessed—that is not something everyone experiences. Except I thought everybody did sense the atmosphere in this way - that when someone else is depressed, you also feel blue.

Learning to hold myself in the depths of feeling what others feel (and having the label empath to go with it); to soothe myself through such painful feelings, was my experiential journey of the next 8 years. Behavioural techniques didn't always help. Psychological tools sometimes did; other times they just made me feel worse.

And on the flip side, when you feel things that deeply, you also have the capacity to feel the same in the opposite direction—such dizzying heights of emotion. I had had glimpses of the highs, but far, far less frequently. Getting praised for my academic success did initially give me such a high. Feeling the expansion and connection at a sunrise Church service on the beach and then later as a teenager, sitting in Circle for a Wiccan Sabbat (on my parent's utility floor), were more enduring examples of riding the higher waves.

Starting yoga was my path back home to myself. The mind-body connection reminded me of the connected expansiveness I felt when in Circle as a teenager. From here, being able to hold space for myself to lean into my emotions and developing a spiritual faith of my own, gifted me a sense of wholeness I had never felt in my life.

My life's path was compounded in all of this, by never truly having made a choice for myself, in what I wanted to do, be, feel, and have. Suggestions from others had led my decisions, never having felt confident enough to make my own. I followed suit, when my first two long-term boyfriends told me they loved me first. I didn't question the prominent, older male colleague who took me for coffee when a job got cancelled and then followed me back to my house-share and tried to kiss me, having been waiting on my bed (clearly wanting more). I had agreed with the tutor who had suggested I become a Sign Language interpreter, without thinking through what I truly wanted.

When I was feeling the indecision of every decision so deeply, the uncertainty of making the wrong choice and the learned conditioning of always putting others needs before my own— looking back I have such compassion for my younger self.

With hindsight, it was unsurprising that my body chose to tell me, in no uncertain terms, that enough was enough. Right after I'd finished my Diploma—the first thing I'd consciously ever chosen solely for myself, cue 2 months off work with debilitating abdominal pain.

I couldn't do anything.

Drugged up on Tramadol and other strong painkillers, for the first time in my life all I could do was feel. The painkillers managed the physical pain, but not all the emotional pain I'd gotten very good at hiding under that metaphorical rug, all these years.

With nothing but time on my hands, I had to learn to lean into what I was feeling. And as I unravelled what I was feeling—some of this done through formal methods such as hypnotherapy and others through my own yoga, breath-work and meditation practices and business learning courses (aka trying to figure out what I wanted to do in the world going forward)—the physical pain started to subside.

My body forced me to take a break—literally stopping my world in its tracks completely for two months and to take a good long look at what I was doing with my life, how I felt about that and what needed to change (once the pain got sorted out). If I hadn't been forced to take those two months off work, in 2018, I would have kept on the path I had been to date—a life where everything was experienced in pastel shades, not the true vibrancy or depth of what I could potentially feel.

Getting dragged out of my busyness forced me to look long and hard in the mirror. Feeling the difference in my physical pain decreasing, as I unravelled my emotions, tied in with the joy and pleasure I experienced in helping other interpreters resolve their work dilemmas in the 1:1 coaching (professional supervision) I was giving them, started to give me clues as to where I was headed.

I kept learning to tune into and follow my intuition over the next 18 months, in which I worked to uncover my emotional hiding tendencies, the business and spiritual courses I enrolled on and leaning into the acceptance that my interpreting career was not going to be for the rest of my life.

I had even presented a paper to an interpreting conference in 2012 about building your house on rocks, not sand—and yet here I was still building on sand, nearly two years after the Universe (and my body) had started to tell me I wasn't on the right path.

And whilst I'd gotten a lot better about listening to myself, working out what was right for me and was working on the side to launch my coaching business, I clearly still hadn't got the message fully! Covid19 hit and at first it kind of felt like a blessing—no more London commute, having the company of living with my boyfriend and the time to focus on getting my first coaching products out the door.

Then I followed the nudges to Glastonbury at the end of August 2020 and my life truly got booted onto my right path. My solo retreat trip to the spiritual heart-centre of the UK (and some say the world) was planned as a 34th birthday treat to myself and my self-initiation weekend, for my upcoming coaching work.

By this point in the summer, I had accepted that my entire meditation process re-writing itself one morning on me, was a clear indicator that the coaching I was meant to launch into the world had to contain the meditations I was receiving and that the spiritual elements that had been crucial in my own acceptance and ease, also needed to be a part of what I offered. Being able to make such decisions, when previously I had always looked to others, gave me the confidence (backed by the expansive intuitive feeling) to know I was on the right path.

Going to Glastonbury changed my life, as whilst the self-initiation ritual I had planned—of immersing myself in The White Spring— didn't come to fruition, (Covid19 had closed it, due to volunteer numbers); what I received instead, was exactly what I needed.

This included the process of learning in the Goddess Temple that my heart was still closed, despite all the emotional work I'd done in the past 18 months; followed by the connection with the crystals shop manager, who followed through on his intuitive knowledge to invite me to return the next day, before I went up Glastonbury Tor. I had brought the rhodonite crystal that had called to me and as I sat in the corner of the shop that next morning, with the other crystals he had me hold, I nearly burst into tears, as my higher heart chakra opened more fully.

Walking the winding sheep trails around and up Glastonbury Tor afterwards, reminded me of reading Priestess initiation rituals that included a similar element in The Mists of Avalon as a teenager and I felt even more of a homecoming as I summited the Tor. Laying atop the Tor, wind blowing fit to bust, with the rhodonite on my breastbone, I underwent the second of my transformative experiences of that weekend—the creation and activation of my Heart's Heart-Light™ Machine. (The first had been my ritual self-initiation bath at my magical AirBnB on my arrival—picked for its supply of candles, essential oil burners and oracle card decks.)

I came back home after that weekend, the most me I had ever been in my life.

Other transformative processes had occurred that weekend. I experienced a past-life cord cutting of my own creation, at the centre of Stonehenge and on my way home, at Avebury Henge, I created and underwent in the same split seconds, two further Heart-Light™ activations. One of the biggest gifts of the weekend was a true sense of peace, calm, knowing, certainty, courage, self-belief and self-trust during my solo time away. And coming from someone who has never felt ok being on her own, it was such a relief to find myself aligned and in flow.

Returning home from that time away was the beginning of the end and the end of my beginning. Very quickly, the gorgeous converted apartment that I owned with my then-boyfriend no longer felt like home. The 10-year relationship we had toasted with champagne and Indian take away earlier that year (well, we were in lockdown) no longer sat right with me.

That weekend at Glastonbury (and its surrounding experiences and connections) was the lightning bolt I'd agreed to, to jump start my life and shine its light on everything that was no longer aligned for me. Everything that I had been ignoring, I no longer could. So, with the strength of my faith as my bedrock, an emotional roller coaster of a fortnight and ALL the signs under the sun slapping me round the face like a wet fish—I knew the right, but not easy, decision for me was to end the relationship and move out.

As soon as the dust settled and the sale was proceeding, I escaped to my own rental place. Being able to lean fully into my spiritual devotions led me to several local hill forts over the next couple of months—Iron Age and Celtic, connecting in with my ancestors and receiving my final 3 Heart-Light™ activations the day before New Year's Eve 2020.

Having my Heart-Light™ process finalised, gave me the opportunity to use my own tools during one of the most turbulent times of my life, gifting me calm, confidence, clarity, certainty and courage. I felt calm in myself, despite the ups and downs. I owned my confidence in my decision making. I was clear in my direction and if my path became unclear, I knew how to tune in and ascertain my direction. And I gained the certainty in my skills that were developing at a pace—I'd always been good at seeing to the heart of the matter for other people, but this was a whole new level of being able to guide others.

The courage was the surprising one. Being courageous enough to end a 10 year relationship with a guy I'd hoped I might marry one day, had not been on the books. Nor was creating a new model of working with your emotions, via your Heart-Light™ Machine, and having the courage to start sharing it with the world as it developed. And stepping out as an author of a chapter in a book titled "Soul Mission" was definitely a leap of courage I would not have taken, not that many months ago. The courage practice below has helped keep me steady as this chapter has taken shape.

Shoring up your courage practice:

Visualise a circular platform radiating out from under your feet, perhaps in stone or a dark red colour. This is your foundation, the base of feeling confident and courageous.

But over time, events, people and places have added to your foundation, building a larger, but uneven platform. Ask now that anything that is not truly a part of your foundation shows itself – by turning a different colour. And now see those sections falling away, so that what is left is truly and confidently you.

Now call together those remaining pieces, into one solid platform beneath your feet – supporting you, gifting you the courage you need going forward.

I share my story to show you that what I once perceived as my greatest weakness, I now utilise as my greatest strength. I have experienced the darkest of my depths, to now be able to soar to such giddy heights of ecstatic joy and bliss that my heart twinges at the heights of happiness I can experience. My sensitivity and depth of feeling are my secret weapons, without which my intuition and spiritual gifts would not be anywhere near as powerful as they are.

I stand for a world where no one else should feel as small, as scared, as anxious and uncertain of themselves as I did. I want to prove that whether you currently feel numb to the emotional rollercoaster, or you feel like you're barely strapped into that first car hurtling its way up and down around the track—you are not the only one.

And it does not have to stay that way.

In owning that I have a fire that burns deep inside me; a Heart-Flame™ that never was truly extinguished, I can now tend it to burn so very brightly and shine my Heart-Light™ to the world. And you too can claim the same joy, peace and certainty for yourself. After all - you are Human. You are Divine. So, from one Heart-Light™ to another, know that it is OK to feel and that you are deeply loved.

ABOUT THE AUTHOR

HANNAH WATSON

Hannah Watson is the Founder and CEO of Hannah Watson Development. She empowers emotionally-frazzled, indecisive and anxious entrepreneurs to be calm, confident, clear, certain and courageous in running their successful online businesses.

As The Elemental Development Guide™ and creator of the Heart-Light; Soul-Ease™ method, Hannah's experience has moulded her holistic skillset crossing many mental, emotional and spiritual elements. This enables her to guide her clients in the exact growth and healing they need, to experience the bliss of effortlessly delivering their gifts to the world.

Hannah lives in the South of England, near to the energies of Avebury henge, Glastonbury and StoneHenge. Being able to regularly connect with her energetic heritage at such sites fuels her work and when she is not trekking up the local Iron Age Hill Fort, she can be found curled up on the sofa under the softest of blankets, book in hand.

Business name: Hannah Watson Development
Website: www.hannahwatsondevelopment.com
Facebook: https://www.facebook.com/HannahWatsonDev
Instagram: @theelementaldevelopmentguide
Email: hi@hannahwatsondevelopment.com

ADAM MENDOZA

ESSENTIALLY YOURS

"Pain Pushes until Vision Pulls" Rev Deborah L Johnson, Inner Light Ministries

Without a doubt, I can attest to 40 plus years of pain. Pain from a failed marriage. Pain from financial ruin. Pain from broken relationships. Pain from endeavors that have fallen short of expectations. The pain of losing loved ones. But as I stand here today, my vision has become clear, and laser-focused. It has pulled me into my life's work.

I started The Bay Area Beat with Rhoda Shapiro in 2019. The goal was to bring stories to the forefront, highlighting community leaders and individuals who were doing the positive, impactful work we hear so little about in conventional news media. As we put it, "Sharing the stories of positive vibrations in the bay area. Stories that reach into the heart of the amazing work being done by communities and individuals all across the bay. Stories of unheralded achievements in education, technology, civic engagement as well as the arts and entertainment that convey the pulse of the bay area's unique diversity. Stories that resonate with cooperation, entrepreneurship and innovation.

I had gone to school to study journalism and longed to be a writer. As luck would have it, I wandered over to the other side of the communications building one day and found a pension for writing ad copy. Thus began a 25 plus career in advertising.

I spent years struggling with demanding clients, impossible deadlines, and trying to navigate Silicon Valley. All the while realizing I was becoming more and more out of alignment, although I did not speak in those terms way back then. Fast forward to 2003, and I received an opportunity to move to Hawaii and manage a start-up retail operation. It was our baby from beginning to end and became one of the most rewarding adventures of my life. But what I learned most was the spirit of Aloha. The spirit of family, sharing, and being of a community. I returned to California to be closer to my children a few years ago and really didn't have much direction for this next chapter.

Soon I realized I had to create this next chapter myself. It became a very difficult road. I freelanced, I did landscaping, I hawked at Christmas in the mall. All while trying to find some direction. I became involved in empowering Latinx high school students through an organization I had done writing for. It was a short contract, and when it ended, I felt my heart burst open, knowing that I could impact lives with my mentoring and professional experience.

At this time, I began to delve into my spiritual awareness and try to find an avenue that encapsulated my total outpouring of empowerment and storytelling. The idea came when I was involved in a student project, organizing declaration days for students in low-income areas that had received scholarships to places like Princeton and Stanford. I was interviewed about that particular event by Rhoda Shapiro, who had started The Milpitas Beat, an off the cuff publication serving a growing and underserved audience. In that moment, I was able to clearly see the vision that would draw on my journalism side as well as my need to share empowered stories with the world. Hence was born The Bay Area Beat. So we gathered the tools to create a podcast, and I tapped into the talent my mother always called "the gift of gab". The process was easy. Find people in their dharma that are making a positive impact in the world and give them the microphone and GO!

Suddenly all these stories and amazing individuals drove me to empower, share, support, and give audience to these folks who were working thanklessly in such an unsung manner.

With each interview, I felt such a true connection between community and partnership. I wanted to string all these good ideas and people together to support and grow in every way imaginable. This is where I find myself today. A de facto Pied Piper of good news. A Troubadour whose song is not mine but belongs to all.

Recently Rhoda has moved on to pursue other areas, and here I am. Alone on this road of redemption and endless possibilities. I honestly don't get hung up on how many listeners we gain every week. I just keep pushing. Keep pushing. It's all I can do. It's in my blood.

The episodes have ranged in topics from historical figures who worked with Cesar Chavez, and continue to work in human rights for Daca and Immigration laws, to homeless advocates and organizations committed to feeding those in need. We have had some fabled musicians and artists sharing their work of community, and we have done it all under one flag. The idea that the local community is where we can make real change in our lives. In a period of political unrest and racial tension, we have focused on the next-door neighbor. We have turned off the corporate broadcast news and have just set up a platform to share positive work. One story at a time.

Subsequently, I have spent the past two years on an amazing spiritual journey. I am purging my old ego ways and tuning into a more divine vibration. No longer fearing truth, I hold honesty and communication near to my core values. Hence, I am now an open book. Quite an entertaining read, if I may say so myself. I've learned to listen, to show compassion, and to breathe in the gratitude that's all around us, even in these crazy times. I perhaps trust too much as I've learned, but it's worth it, acceptance of all things on my journey. I feel and am exposed to a lot of love in my heart.

So what does that look like today? Our world, frozen in the throws of a pandemic. The once festive gatherings that brought like-minded spirits together, relegated to quiet bedrooms and dens on Zoom calls. And me, working as a manager now at Trader Joes. An essential worker. But I know deep down, the essential part of my journey lies beyond the store's doors 40-50 hours a week. I have had to become a social worker, guru, nutritionist, and friend to neighbors frightened on their only trip outside their homes in weeks. The elderly are the most vulnerable. They are confused, hungry, scared. And so that role I relish, of bringing good news to the community has taken shape in yet another form.

Honestly, the work at the store has kept me busy, and I am now able to get back to spreading the good news.

I see now how so many have been impacted by this terrible pandemic. I'm in a position to help as best as I can, and so it is. I have taken it upon myself to build real meaningful relationships with our community, in store and out. I knew that my previous experience sharing Aloha on the islands in retail would serve me well at one of the few mainland companies that practice that Hawaiian spirit. That spirit grows stronger every day as I became more confident in knowing jams from preserves and arugula from kale.

I would say I've poured my heart into this job, but I haven't had to. My heart has been in this job since day one. It just flows. Fast forward to where we find ourselves today, deemed essential workers. At last, credibility for what I call, The Nobility of the Grocer.

The truth is, I have gotten more than one story from the checkout stand. It has helped even further strengthen my belief in community. As I dive deeper into my spirituality, and away from the material bubble of the Silicon Valley, it's become abundantly clear that food and spirit are energy sources. The positive experience of procuring that food source translates to dinner tables everywhere. The love and energy of our stores leave a lasting impression on our customers. A loving energy that doesn't end when we hand them their receipt.

As host of The Bay Area Beat, I have been privileged to have interviewed such a wide variety of guests. My very first guest was a young woman who ran across the US on foot to raise awareness of injured student-athletes. Athletes who were at risk of losing scholarships and their entire academic future due to sports-related injuries. We held a conversation while she was in the middle of Indiana. She completed her journey, and I am so grateful for the community and technology that brought me this inspirational story. I've interviewed community group leaders, artist movements, young entrepreneurs, and teachers of all walks of life. All with a story to empower the world around them. For me, it has been a true inspiration. One story at a time.

I spend my nights bringing joyful culinary communion to the good people of Los Gatos CA. and spend my days writing and working on my labor of love, The Bay Area Beat. I get to do these amazing interviews and share stories that feature guests who resonate all that I am in my life right now.

When I attended my first Public Relations course in college, my professor made it clear that PR was not about liking people. I remember feeling a bit uneasy because I wanted to work in the public and make positive change way back then. Well, 30 plus years and countless resume revisions later, I've found my place where it's all about liking people. Happy people doing what makes people happy.

With this whole Covid-19 thing, we've had to go above and beyond to keep people safe. Today was rough, we are all feeling the stress of uncertainty, and no one is immune to a mini meltdown these days. I could have done better today. I will do better tomorrow. I'm in a place that feels like home. I call it my happy place.

I lead a dual life but with equal passion and purpose. I've gotten some of my best podcast leads at the checkout stand. It's in the conversations, it's in the brainstorming, and it's in the shared passions. It's all about connecting for that divine purpose.

We all know we've made a quantum leap in our world over the past few weeks and months. Tomorrow will not be the same. My wish is that we all awaken to our heart's calling and listen to what we have always longed for in our lives. Slow down, sample life, take the time to talk to our neighbors, and be patient with each other.

That's the journey. And this I've learned. Be a good person. Listen to others. Listen to your heart. Use every moment as an opportunity to teach and share. Know that in your heart, the world has a place to be a universe of loving perfection. It may not be your responsibility to make others feel the same, but you can shine your light and ignite the light of those who may have been dimmed. You can start by being mindful of toxic traits like Blame, Fear, Judgement, and, most importantly, Anger. Sit in meditation every morning and call love into your heart. Lastly, the most important lesson I've learned from Rev Deborah Johnson, who I mentioned in the opening, is this: As humans and children of God, we are verbs, not nouns. We are in constant motion, and change is in our nature. And I am so very blessed to be "Adaming" through life these days.

ABOUT THE AUTHOR

ADAM MENDOZA

Adam Mendoza is a freelance writer for national and local publications. Originally from Los Angeles CA, he studied Journalism at San Jose State from 1982-1986.

Recently, he has been working with educators and recruitment professionals featuring high achieving youth in lower economic and at risk areas in a positive and empowering light through various media platforms.

The Bay Area Beat is a weekly Podcast dedicated to sharing positive stories of achievement in The Bay Area and beyond. Stories that reach into the heart of the amazing work being done by communities and individuals all across the bay. Stories of unheralded achievements in education, technology, civic engagement as well as the arts and entertainment that convey the pulse of the bay area's unique diversity. Stories that resonate cooperation, entrepreneurship and innovation.

Bay Area Beat is a podcast airing Wednesdays at 10:00 am Hosted by Adam Mendoza
Website: www.thebayareabeat.com

ABOUT THE PUBLISHER

House of Indigo provides soulful leaders opportunities to stand out in their industries. Through amplifying the reach of purpose-driven individuals, they are able to be seen by readers who will be connected to their expertise, message and work, resulting in inspiration, impact and influential changes.

At House of Indigo, it is our mission to provide ways for leaders to emerge, increase visibility and leverage their expertise through various media opportunities including book publications, immersions and courses. The ripple effect of impact that is created when each person rises up and shares their story and lessons is profound. We are here to support that ripple into becoming a tsunami. The more conscious expanding tools we provide, the closer we get.

We are always looking for more contributors for multi-authored books, solo published books, immersions, classes and more. If you have a story or teaching in you that is waiting to be unleashed, we'd love to hear from you.

house-indigo.com
jessverrill.com
Facebook Group: The Indigo Initiative

Printed in Great Britain
by Amazon